UNDER SENTENCE OF DEATH

by

VICTOR HUGO

Copyright © 2016 Read Books Ltd.
This book is copyright and may not be
reproduced or copied in any way without
the express permission of the publisher in writing

British Library Cataloguing-in-Publication Data
A catalogue record for this book is available from
the British Library

CONTENTS

Victor Hugo. 5
CHAPTER I. 11
CHAPTER II. 13
CHAPTER III. 19
CHAPTER IV. 20
CHAPTER V. 20
CHAPTER VI. 22
CHAPTER VII. 24
CHAPTER VIII. 25
CHAPTER IX. 26
CHAPTER X. 27
CHAPTER XI. 28
CHAPTER XII. 30
CHAPTER XIII. 32
CHAPTER XIV. 39
CHAPTER XV. 42
CHAPTER XVI. 43
CHAPTER XVII. 44
CHAPTER XVIII. 44
CHAPTER XIX. 45
CHAPTER XX. 46
CHAPTER XXI. 48
CHAPTER XXII. 54
CHAPTER XXIII. 59
CHAPTER XXIV. 60
CHAPTER XXV. 61
CHAPTER XXVI. 62
CHAPTER XXVII. 63
CHAPTER XXVIII. 63

CHAPTER XXIX...67
CHAPTER XXX,,,,,,,,,,, ...68
CHAPTER XXXI..70
CHAPTER XXXII..73
CHAPTER XXXIII..74
CHAPTER XXXIV..74
CHAPTER XXXV..75
CHAPTER XXXVI..76
CHAPTER XXXVII..76
CHAPTER XXXVIII..77
CHAPTER XXXIX..78
CHAPTER XL..80
CHAPTER XLI..82
CHAPTER XLII..85
CHAPTER XLIII..86
CHAPTER XLIV..86
CHAPTER XLV..87
CHAPTER XLVI..87

Victor Hugo

Victor Marie Hugo was born on 26th February 1802, in Besançon, Franche-Comté, France. He was a political campaigner, artist, poet, novelist and dramatist of the Romantic movement, considered one of the greatest French writers of all time.

Hugo's father was a freethinking republican who considered Napoléon a hero, and his mother was a Catholic Royalist, who was executed in 1812 for plotting against the legendary general. Hugo's childhood was a period of national political turmoil. Napoléon was proclaimed Emperor two years after Hugo's birth, and the Bourbon Monarchy was restored before his eighteenth birthday. The opposing political and religious views of Hugo's parents reflected the forces that would battle for supremacy in France throughout his life.

As a young man, his mother dominated his education and upbringing, and as a result Hugo's early work in poetry and fiction reflects her passionate devotion to both King and Faith. It was only later, during the events leading up to France's 1848 Revolution, that he would begin to rebel against his Catholic Royalist education and instead champion Republicanism and Freethought. Hugo was also a rebellious young man, and on falling in love with his childhood friend Adèle Foucher (1803–

1868), became secretly engaged against his mothers wishes. Because of his close relationship with his mother, Hugo waited until after his mother's death (in 1821) to marry Adèle in 1822.

Hugo published his first novel the year following his marriage (*Han d'Islande*, 1823), and his second three years later (*Bug-Jargal*, 1826). Between 1829 and 1840 he would publish five more volumes of poetry, cementing his reputation as one of the greatest elegiac and lyric poets of his time. Victor Hugo's first mature work of fiction appeared in 1829, and reflected the acute social conscience that would infuse his later work. *The Last Day of a Condemned Man* would have a profound influence on later writers such as Albert Camus, Charles Dickens, and Fyodor Dostoevsky. It was soon followed by *The Hunchback of Notre-Dame* (in 1831), which was quickly translated into other language across Europe.

Adèle and Victor Hugo had their first child, Léopold, in 1823, but the boy died in infancy. The following year, on 28th August 1824, the couple's second child, Léopoldine was born, followed by Charles in 1826, François-Victor in 1828, and Adèle in 1830. Hugo's oldest and favourite daughter, Léopoldine, died at the age of nineteen in 1843, shortly after her marriage to Charles Vacquerie. On 4th September 1843, she drowned in the Seine at Villequier, pulled down by her heavy skirts, when a boat overturned. Her young husband also died trying to save her. The death left her father devastated; Hugo was travelling with his mistress at the time in the south of France, and first learned about Léopoldine's death from a newspaper he read in a cafe.

Hugo wrote many poems about his daughter's tragic life and death, and many biographers have claimed that he never completely recovered from this traumatic incident. His most famous poem is probably *Demain, Dès L'aube*, in which he describes visiting her grave. He began planning a major novel about social misery and injustice as early as the 1830s, but it would take a full seventeen years for *Les Misérables* to be realized and finally published in 1862. On its publication, the critical establishment was generally hostile to the novel, with Gustave Flaubert claiming he found within it 'neither truth nor greatness' and Baudelaire castigating it as 'tasteless and inept.' Despite this, *Les Misérables* was a massive hit with the public, and today remains Victor Hugo's most enduringly popular work.

After three unsuccessful attempts, Hugo was finally elected to the Académie Française in 1841, solidifying his position in the world of French arts and letters. He was also elevated to the peerage by King Louis-Philippe in the same year and entered the Higher Chamber as a *pair de France*, where he spoke against the death penalty and social injustice, and in favour of freedom of the press and self-government for Poland. In 1848, Hugo was elected to the Parliament as a conservative. In 1849 he broke with the conservatives when he gave a noted speech calling for the end of misery and poverty. When Louis Napoleon (Napoleon III) seized complete power in 1851, establishing an anti-parliamentary constitution, Hugo openly declared him a traitor to France.

Hugo decided to live in exile after Napoleon III's coup d'état at the end of 1851. After leaving France, he lived in Brussels briefly in 1851, before moving to the Channel Islands, first to Jersey (1852–1855) and then to the smaller island of Guernsey in 1855, where he stayed until 1870. Whilst in exile, Hugo published his famous political pamphlets against Napoleon

III, *Napoléon le Petit* and *Histoire d'un Crime*, which whilst banned in France, had a strong impact. Although Napoleon III proclaimed a general amnesty in 1859, the author stayed in exile, only returning when Napoleon was forced from power in 1870. Hugo's next novel, *Troilers of the Sea* turned away from the social and political themes so prevalent in *Les Miserables*. It told the story of a man hoping to gain the approval of his beloved's father by rescuing his ship - thus battling the elements, mythical beasts and the sea itself. It was published in 1866, and was dedicated to the channel islands, in which Hugo found such a welcoming home.

Hugo returned to political and social issues in his next novel, *The Man Who Laughs*, which was published in 1869 and painted a critical picture of the aristocracy. The novel was not as successful as his previous efforts, and Hugo himself began to comment on the growing distance between himself and literary contemporaries such as Flaubert and Émile Zola, whose realist and naturalist novels were now exceeding the popularity of his own work. After the Siege of Paris, Hugo lived again in Guernsey from 1872 to 1873, before finally returning to France for the remainder of his life. His last novel, *Ninety-Three*, published in 1874, dealt with a subject that Hugo had previously avoided: the Reign of Terror during the French Revolution. Though Hugo's popularity was on the decline at the time of its publication, many now consider *Ninety-Three* to be a work on par with his earlier and better-known novels.

When Hugo returned to Paris in 1870, the country hailed him as a national hero. This was a sad time for the ageing writer however, as within a brief period he suffered a mild stoke, his daughter Adèle's internment in an insane asylum, and the death of his two sons. His wife Adèle had died in 1868. Hugo's mistress, Juliette Drouet, also died in 1883 – two years before Hugo's own death. Despite this, to honour the fact that he was entering his eightieth year, in 1882, one of the greatest tributes to a living writer was held. The celebrations began on 25th June when Hugo was presented with a Sèvres vase, the traditional gift for sovereigns, and on 27th June one of the largest parades in French history was held.

Victor Hugo's death from pneumonia on 22nd May 1885, at the age of eighty-three, generated intense national mourning. He was not only revered as a towering figure in literature, but he was also a statesman who shaped the Third Republic and democracy in France. More than two million people joined his funeral procession in Paris from the Arc de Triomphe to the Panthéon, where he was buried. He shares a crypt within the with Alexandre Dumas and Émile Zola.

UNDER SENTENCE OF DEATH

CHAPTER I.

Sentenced to death!

For five whole weeks have I lived with this one thought, always alone with it, always frozen by its ghastly presence, always crushed beneath its overwhelming weight.

At first, years ago, as it seemed, not mere weeks as it really was, I was a man like any other. Every day, every hour, every minute was ruled by its own idea. My intellect, young and fresh, lost itself in a world of fantasy. I amused myself in mapping out a life without order, and without end, weaving into a thousand fantastic patterns the coarse and slender tissue of my existence. There were lovely girls, cardinals' copes, victories won, theatres full of life and light, and then again the young girls, and walks in the twilight under the spreading boughs of the chestnut trees. My imagination always pictured scenes of pleasure. My thoughts were free, and therefore I was free also.

But now I am a prisoner. My body is in irons in a dungeon,

and my soul is fettered by an idea—one horrible, murderous, and implacable idea. I have but one thought, one certainty, one deep-rooted conviction, and that is that I am under sentence of death!

Do what I may, that one terrible thought is ever with me, like a spectre by my side, lonely and jealous, driving away every effort that I may make to liberate myself from its presence, face to face with me, and clutching me with its icy hand when I endeavour to turn aside my head, or to close my eyes upon its horrifying existence.

It intrudes itself into all the thoughts by which I vainly strive to forget it; I hear it like a horrible chorus in every word that is addressed to me; it places its face against mine as I glance through the barred windows of my dungeon; it attacks me whilst waking, it haunts my spasmodic efforts at sleep, and appears in my dreams under the form of the axe of the guillotine.

It is still present as I wake up with a start, and say, "It is but a dream." Well, even before my eyes have had time to open, and to see the whole terrible reality which surrounds me, written on the damp stone of my prison walls, in the pale rays of my lamp, in the coarse fabric of my clothes, in the dark figure of the sentinel whose bayonet gleams through the loophole of my dungeon, it seems as if a sonorous voice murmurs in my ears:

"*Sentenced to death!*"

CHAPTER II.

It was a lovely morning in August.

Three days had passed since my trial had been commenced; three days since my crime had collected every morning a crowd of curious spectators, who lounged on the benches of the court like carrion crows around a carcase; three days since that strange, half visionary procession of judges, of lawyers, of witnesses, and public prosecutors, had passed and repassed before me, sometimes ludicrous, but always murderous, always gloomy and fatal.

During the first two nights restlessness and nervousness had prevented me from sleeping; on the third, weariness and lassitude had conduced to slumber. At midnight I had left the jury still deliberating. Re-conducted to my cell, I had thrown myself on my pallet, and had fallen at once into a deep sleep—the sleep of forgetfulness. It was my first repose for many days. I was still wrapped in this profound slumber when they came and woke me. This time the tramp of the gaoler's heavy shoes, the clink of his bunch of keys, and the harsh grating of the bolts, were not sufficient to arouse me from my stupor; he had to shake me, and to shout in my ear—"Get up!"

I opened my eyes, and with a bound rose from my couch. At that instant, through the narrow window pierced in the higher portion of the walls of my cell, I saw reflected upon the ceiling of the adjoining passage (the only means by which I could catch a glimpse of the sky), the sun. I love the sunlight.

"It is a fine day," remarked I to the gaoler.

He remained silent for an instant, as though considering whether it were worth while to reply to me; then, as though making an effort, he answered sullenly—

"Yes, it seems so."

I remained motionless, my intellectual powers almost dormant, and my eyes fixed upon that soft golden reflection that gilded the ceiling.

"It is a lovely day," repeated I.

"Yes," answered the man, "but they are waiting for you."

These few words, like the web of the spider that intercepts the flight of the fly, threw me roughly back into every-day life. On a sudden I again saw, as in a flash of lightning, the court of justice, the table before the judges, strewn with blood-stained rags, the three ranks of witnesses with their expressionless faces, the two gendarmes at each side of the dock, the black gowns of the bar constantly moving to and fro, the heads of the crowd thronged together in the body of the court, and the fixed gaze of the twelve jurymen, who had watched whilst I had slept.

I rose up, my teeth chattered, my hands trembled so that I could hardly gather together my clothes, my legs bent under me. At the first step that I attempted to take I staggered like a porter whose load is too heavy for him. However, I nerved myself, and followed my gaoler.

The two gendarmes were waiting for me on the threshold of my cell. They handcuffed me again. It was rather a complicated lock, which they had some trouble in closing. I submitted passively—it was a machine put into a machine.

We passed through one of the inner courtyards; the fresh

air of the morning gave me strength. I raised my head. The sky was of a bright blue, and the warm sunbeams, broken by the lofty chimneys, traced great angular lines of light on the tall and gloomy walls of the prison. In truth it was very beautiful.

We mounted a spiral staircase, we passed through one corridor, then another, and again through a third; then a low door was opened. A warm breath of air, and the sound of voices met me; it was the murmuring of the crowd in the court. I entered.

On my appearance there was a clang of arms and a confused sound of voices, seats were noisily pushed aside, and as I passed through the long room between the lines of spectators, kept in position by soldiers, it seemed as if I were the centre point upon which every eye was fixed.

At that instant I perceived that my irons had been removed, but when and how I knew not.

Then there was a deep silence. I had reached my appointed place. As the disturbance ceased in the crowd, so my ideas grew clearer. I understood what I had before only vaguely surmised—that the decisive moment had arrived, and that I had been brought into court to hear my sentence.

Explain it as you may, when this idea entered my head I felt no fear. The windows of the court were wide open, the fresh air and the busy hum of the city poured in freely; the court was as neatly arranged as if it was to be the place in which a marriage was to be celebrated; the bright rays of the sun traced here and there the luminous shadows of the casements, sometimes spread upon the floor, sometimes portrayed on the tables, now and then broken by the angles of the walls; whilst the beams themselves, shining through the panes of glass, looked like great bars of golden dust. The judges at the end of the room wore a self-satisfied air—no doubt pleased that their task was so nearly concluded. The face of the President, upon which the reflection of one of the panes of glass shone, was calm and benevolent, whilst one of his younger colleagues played with his cap as he conversed gaily with a young lady in a pink bonnet, for whom he had procured a seat just behind himself. The jury alone looked pale and worn out, evidently from having remained awake during the long watches of the night; some of them were yawning. The expression of their faces gave no indication that they felt the responsibility of the sentence that they were about to pronounce, the only noticeable point amongst these worthy shopkeepers being an evident desire for sleep.

Exactly opposite to me was a tall window wide open. Through it I could hear the laughter of the stall-keepers on the quays, and in a crevice in the window-sill was a pretty little yellow floweret waving to and fro in the wind.

How, in the midst of all these pleasing objects, could any unpleasant idea intrude itself? With the balmy air, and the bright sun playing around me, it was impossible to think of anything else except liberty. Hope shone round me like the sunbeams; and in full confidence I awaited my sentence with the feelings of a man looking forward to life and freedom. And now my counsel arrived; he had evidently been breakfasting luxuriously. We were waiting for him. As he moved into his place, he bent towards me, and whispered—

"I have hope still."

"Indeed," answered I, in the same light tone, with a smile on my lips.

"Yes," returned he; "I do not yet know what line the

prosecution will take, but if they cannot prove premeditation, you will only get penal servitude for life."

"How, sir!" exclaimed I, indignantly. "Sooner death a thousand times."

Yes, death. And besides, an inner voice kept repeating to me that I risked nothing by saying this. Who ever heard of sentence of death being pronounced except at midnight, with burning torches, in a damp and gloomy hall, and on a cold and rainy winter's night! But in the month of August, on so beautiful a day, at eight o'clock in the morning, those benevolent-looking jurymen could not have the heart to find me guilty! And my eyes again fixed themselves on the little yellow floweret in the sun light.

At that moment the President, who had been waiting for my counsel, ordered me to stand up. The guard carried arms. As if by a shock of electricity, all those assembled in the court became animated with life. A mean-looking man, seated at a table beneath the judge's chair, evidently the clerk of the court, broke the silence by reading the verdict of the jury, which they had given in my absence. A cold sweat bedewed all my limbs, and I leaned against the wall to save myself from falling.

"Counsel, have you anything to urge against the sentence of death being pronounced?" asked the President.

I could have said a great deal, but I was unable to frame a consecutive sentence; my tongue clove to the roof of my mouth.

My counsel rose to his feet.

As I followed his line of argument I understood that he was endeavouring to soften the verdict of the jury, and striving to induce the judge to inflict the lighter penalty, the penalty which I had been so wounded at his suggesting. My indignation must have been very strong to pierce through the numerous complications of my faculties.

I endeavoured to repeat in a loud voice the words I had already said, "Sooner death a thousand times!" but all that I could do was to clutch him convulsively by the arm, and cry out in convulsive accents, "No, no!"

The Public Prosecutor argued against my counsel's plea, and I listened to him with an air of stupid satisfaction. Then the judges left the court to consult together, and on their return the President read the sentence.

"Condemned to death," murmured the spectators; and as they hurried me away the crowd pressed around me with a noise like that of a falling house. I walked along passively, stupefied and confused.

A sudden transformation had taken place in me. Until the sentence of death had been actually passed, I felt that I was living and breathing like other men; now I felt that a barrier had been erected between myself and my fellow-creatures. Nothing now wore the same aspect as it had done previously. Those tall, luminous windows, the bright sunlight, the clear sky, the beautiful flowers, all became white and pallid like the colour of a shroud. Those men and women and children who pressed around me had something of the air of spectres.

A carriage painted a dirty black, with bars to the windows, was waiting for me. As I was about to enter it, I paused, and looked around me. "A condemned criminal!" cried the passers-by, as they hurried towards the vehicle. Through the mist that seemed to interpose between the world and myself I could perceive the young girls who followed my every movement with greedy eyes.

"Good!" cried the younger one, clapping her hands. "It will be in six weeks' time!"

CHAPTER III.

Condemned to death.

Well, why not? have I not read in some book that *all men are condemned to death with a respite the date of which is not fixed?*

How, then, is my position changed?

Since the day that my sentence was pronounced, how many are dead who had arranged for a long and happy life; how many of those, young, free, and in good health, who expected to see my head fall in the Place de Grêve, have gone before me; and how many more are there, who breathe the free air, and go where they please, who will also precede me to the next world? And why should I long for life? In fact, the prison with its gloomy light, and the black bread which constitutes the prison fare; the thin soup drank from a galley-slave's cup; to be constantly insulted—I, who am refined by education, to be abused by gaolers and by the convict guards; never to see a human being who considers me worthy of a kind word—these are the sole pleasures of life which the executioner will take from me.

And yet it is very terrible!

CHAPTER IV.

The black carriage has brought me here to the hideous prison of the Bicêtre.

Seen from afar, this building has a certain majestic air about it. It is situated at the foot of a hill, and covers a large extent of ground. Looked at from a distance, it retains some of its ancient splendour as a king's palace, but as you come nearer to it the building changes into a mere commonplace edifice. The broken turrets wound the eye. There is an air of shame and degradation about it; it seems as if the walls were struck with the leprosy of crime.

No windows, no glass in the frames, but massive crossed bars of iron, through which can occasionally be seen the pallid countenance of a convict or of a madman. Such is the appearance of the prison when seen closely.

CHAPTER V.

Scarcely had I arrived when I was seized in its iron embraces. Every precaution was multiplied; no knife, no fork was permitted for my meals; the strait-waistcoat, a kind of coarse canvas sack, imprisoned my arms. They were responsible for my life.

I was to be with them for six or seven weeks, and it was their duty to deliver me safe and sound to the executioner.

For the first few days they treated me with a tenderness that had something revolting in it. The kindnesses of a turnkey remind you of the scaffold. But to my delight, after a few days had passed away, custom resumed its sway, and they treated me with the same brutality that they did the other prisoners, and ceased those unusual demonstrations of courtesy which reminded me every moment of the executioner.

My youth, my good behaviour, my attention to the gaol chaplain, and especially a word or two of Latin which I addressed to the porter, who did not understand them, by the way, gave me the privilege of outdoor exercise every week with the other prisoners, and released me from the terrible straitwaistcoat which paralyzed my every movement. After a great deal of hesitation I was permitted the use of pen, ink, and paper, as well as a lamp in the evenings. Every Sunday, after hearing mass, I was permitted to go into the courtyard during the hour devoted to exercise. There I had long conversations with the prisoners. Why not? They are good enough fellows, these poor wretches. They told me what crimes they had committed. At first I was horrified, but after a time I found out that they were given to boasting. They taught me to talk slang, *patter-flash*, as they called it. Thieves' slang is a perfect language grafted on to our expressions of every-day life, a species of hideous excrescence like some loathsome worm. When you first hear this language spoken you instinctively experience a feeling of repulsion as when you see a bundle of foul and dirty rags shaken before you.

But these men pitied me, and they were the only ones who did so. As for the warders, the turnkeys, and the gaolers, I scorned their pity, for they would talk and laugh about me to my very face as though I were some inanimate object.

CHAPTER VI.

I said to myself, "Since I have been furnished with the means of writing, why should I not use them? But what shall I write?" Shut up between four cold and naked stone walls, with no liberty for my feet, no vista for my eyes to range, my sole occupation to follow the slow movement of the white square of light, which, falling through the wicket in my cell door, seemed chiselled in the dark wall of my prison, and, as I said before, alone with one remembrance, the remembrance of a crime and its punishment, of murder, and of death—what have I to say, I who have no longer part and parcel in this world? And how will this shattered brain enable me to write anything worth reading?

But why not? Even though all around me is sombre and out of gear, is there not in me a tempest, a struggle, a tragedy? This fixed idea that holds me in its power, does it not present itself to me each hour in a different shape, in a novel form, and each one more hideous and blood-stained than the one that preceded it? Why should I not endeavour to speak to myself of all the terrible and hitherto unknown sensation that I experience in the desolate position in which I am. Assuredly there is ample material, and though my days are numbered, yet there is enough of anguish, terror, and torture in these last hours of mine to wear out the pen and to empty the inkstand.

Besides, the only method in which I can allay my torments is to observe them closely. The mere fact of describing them will give me repose.

And then what I write will not be without its use. This record of my sufferings hour by hour, and minute by minute, punishment heaped on punishment, if I have the strength to carry it up to that point where it will be *physically* impossible for me to continue it further—this history, unfinished as it necessarily must be, but as complete as I can make it, will it not be well worthy of perusal? Will not this vivid reproduction of agonizing thoughts in that ever-increasing torrent of grief, in that intellectual dissection of the last hours of a man sentenced to death—will it not, I say, contain a striking lesson for those who have condemned him? Perhaps it will make them think twice ere they again consign the living, breathing head of a man to the hands of the executioner. Perhaps, unhappy wretches, they have never considered the slow torture which follows a condemnation to death.

Has the idea never struck them that in the man whom they are going to suppress there is a reasoning intelligence, an intelligence that had counted on a prolonged life, a soul which was not prepared for death? No; they only see in all this the vertical fall of the triangular blade, and doubtless consider that for the condemned man there is neither past nor future.

But my pages will undeceive them. Some day, perhaps, they will be printed, and those who read them will pause for a few moments in this record of a soul's sufferings which they had up to that time never even suspected. They were proud to be able to kill the body with the smallest amount of physical pain. But what good is that? What is physical, when compared with mental pain? A day will come when, perhaps, these memoirs, the last impressions of an unhappy man, may have contributed——Unless, indeed, after my death the wind may toss about the courtyard a few pieces of paper stained with mud, or else, pasted in a broken pane of glass in the porter's lodge, they may serve to exclude the rain.

CHAPTER VII.

And suppose what I have written may be one day of use to others, and may cause the judge to hesitate to doom a fellow-creature to death, that it may save other unfortunates, innocent or guilty, from the agonies to which I am condemned—what good will all this do to me? When my head has been cut off, what does it matter whether they cut off those of others or not? Can I really have been troubling myself about such follies? What good will it do me to abolish the scaffold after I have suffered upon it? What! am I to lose the sun, the spring, the fields full of flowers, the birds which wake up and chirp in the early morning, the clouds, nature, liberty, and life?

Ah! it is myself that I must save. Is it really true that this cannot be done? that I may be taken out and killed to-morrow, to-day, even, for all that I know? The thought is enough to make me dash out my brains against the wall of my cell.

CHAPTER VIII.

Let me count how much time remains to me.

Three days of delay after sentence has been given, to enable me to appeal in.

Eight days of forgetfulness in the office of the court, after which the statement of the case will be sent to the Minister.

Fifteen days waiting at the Minister's, who does not even know that the affair is before him, and yet he is supposed to send it up to the Court of Appeal after examining it. Then it has to be classed, numbered, and registered; for there is plenty of work for the guillotine, and each one must await his turn.

Fifteen days of watching and waiting.

At last the Court of Appeal assembles—generally upon a Thursday—and rejects twenty appeals in a lump, and sends all the papers to the Minister, who sends them to the Public Prosecutor, who communicates with the executioner. Three days.

On the morning of the fourth day the assistant to the Public Prosecutor says to himself, as he ties his neckcloth, "It is time that this affair was finished." Then, if the assistant to the clerk of the court has not a few friends to breakfast who prevent him from attending to his duties, the order for the execution is noted, dated, registered, and sent out, and the next morning, at the break of day, a scaffold is erected in the Place de Grêve, and all through the city are heard the hoarse voices of the newsvendors calling out a full, true, and particular account of the execution. And all this in six weeks! That young girl was right.

So that five weeks, perhaps six, remain; but I dare not rely upon this, and I am in a cell in the Bicêtre, and it seems to me that Thursday has passed three days ago.

CHAPTER IX.

I am going to make my will; but no, it is useless. I am condemned to pay the costs of the trial, and all that I possess will hardly be sufficient to meet the expenses.

The guillotine is an expensive luxury.

I have a mother, a wife, and a child.

A little girl three years of age, gentle, rosy, and delicate, with large black eyes and long chestnut hair.

She was just two years and a month old when I last saw her.

Thus, after my death there will be three women without son, husband, or father; three orphans of different kinds, three widows made by the hand of the law.

I allow that I am justly punished; but what have *these* innocent creatures done? No; these are dishonoured and ruined for no fault of their own: and this is justice!

It is not the thought of my poor old mother that disquiets me; she is sixty-four; the blow will kill her at once, or even if she lingers on for a little while, as long as she has a little fire to warm her feet at she will not complain.

Nor am I uneasy regarding my wife; she is an invalid, and her mind is not very strong; she will die too.

Unless, indeed, she goes mad. They say that mad people live a long while; but if her intellect goes she will not suffer: she will sleep, she is as good as dead.

But my daughter, my child, my poor little Marie, who laughs and plays, who even now, perhaps, is singing and thinking of nothing—that is what cuts me to the heart.

CHAPTER X.

This is what my cell is like:

Eight feet square, four walls of hewn stone standing at right angles upon a flooring of flagstones raised a few inches above the exterior corridor.

On the right-hand side of the door as you enter is a kind of recess, a sort of burlesque alcove. A heap of straw has been thrown into it, on which the prisoner is expected to repose and sleep, clad in his canvas trousers and linen frock, winter and summer.

Above my head, instead of the skies of heaven, is an arched roof, from which hang huge spiders' webs like masses of rags.

No window, not even a loophole, and a door the woodwork of which is hidden by its massive iron plates. No window? I am in error. Towards the top of the door is an opening nine inches square, with a grating over it which the gaoler can close at night.

Outside is a long passage, lighted and ventilated by narrow loopholes high up in the wall, and divided into stone compartments which communicate with each other by a series of low doors. Each of these compartments serves as a kind of ante-chamber to a cell similar to mine. It is in these dungeons that convicts who have infringed the gaol regulations are confined. The three first cells are reserved for criminals condemned to death, as they are nearer to the prison, and therefore more convenient for the officials.

These dungeons are the remains of the ancient castle of Bicêtre, built by the Cardinal of Winchester, the same priest who ordered Jeanne d'Arc to be burnt alive. I heard the gaoler telling this to some anxious sightseers who came and stared at me in my dungeon as if I was a beast in a menagerie. I should add that a sentinel is always on guard at the door of the cell, and that whenever my gaze falls upon the opening in the door it meets two widely opened eyes fixed intently upon mine. I believe that it is supposed that there is both air and light in the stone box in which I am confined.

CHAPTER XI.

As daylight has not yet come, what shall I do with the hours of the night? An idea has struck me: I have risen, and moved my lamp along the four walls of my cell. They are covered with writing, drawings, designs, and strange figures of all kinds. It seems as if each condemned prisoner had resolved here at least to leave some remembrance of himself, either in chalk or charcoal, in white or black letters, sometimes deeply graven in the stone, at other times rusty-looking, as though traced in blood. If my mind was more at ease I should take great interest in this strange book which opens its leaves before my eyes on every stone of my dungeon. I should have liked to have collected together all these fragments of thought scattered about on the walls, to have picked out the inscriptions of each man, and to have given sense and life to all these mutilated sentences, to these dismembered phrases, to these half-finished words, heads without bodies, like those who had carved them on the walls.

A little above my bed were two bleeding hearts pierced with an arrow, and above it was *Love for Life*: the unhappy man had not had his wish gratified. By the side of this was a sort of three-cornered hat, and underneath this a small figure clumsily executed, with these words, *Long live the Emperor, 1824*.

Again, I noticed the burning hearts with this motto: *I love Mathias Dunvin-Jacques*. On the opposite wall was the word *Papavoine*, the P covered with elaborate arabesques and flourishes; next to it were a few verses of an obscene song. A cap of Liberty deeply cut into the stone, with the name, *Bovies—The Republic*. This was the name of one of the non-commissioned officers of La Rochelle. Poor young fellow! How hideous are the pretended necessities of political intrigue, to risk for an idea, for a dream, that terrible reality, the guillotine, and I, who pity myself, miserable wretch, I have committed a real crime, and have spilt blood!

I did not continue my researches, for drawn in white, in a dark corner of the room, I saw an appalling design; it was a representation of that scaffold which may even now be in course of erection for me. My lamp almost fell from my hands.

CHAPTER XII.

I turned away and sat down on my bed, my face buried in my hands, and my elbows resting on my knees; my childish fright had passed away, and a strange desire had taken possession of me to continue my researches.

By the side of the name of Papavoine I tore away a large spider's web covered with dust, and stretched across the angle of the wall; under it were four names, easy to decipher: Dantun, 1815; Poulain, 1818; Jean Martin, 1821; Castaing, 1823. As I read these names a flood of horrible recollections pounced upon me: Dantun had cut up his brother, and, going about Paris by night, had thrown his head into a well, and the limbs and trunk into different portions of the sewers. Poulain had murdered his wife. Jean Martin had fired a pistol at his father as the old man was looking out of a window. Castaing was a doctor, who had poisoned his friend, and whilst attending to him professionally gave him fresh doses of poison. Whilst Papavoine was a horrible maniac, who slew little children with knife-thrusts in the head. "These," thought I, as a feverish shiver shook me—"these have been the denizens of this cell before me; it is here, on this very floor, that they, men of blood and slaughter, have thought out their last thoughts; it is in this narrow space that they have paced up and down like savage beasts." They succeeded each other with great rapidity; this cell does not remain empty long. They have left the nest warm, and it is to me that they have left it. I, in my turn, shall join them in the cemetery of Clamont, where the grass grows so luxuriantly and well. I am not a visionary, nor am I superstitious; it is probable that these gloomy thoughts produced a slight attack of fever, for whilst I was thus musing it seemed to me as if these fatal names were written in fire on the black wall; I heard a buzzing in my ears, which grew quicker and quicker; a red light shone in my eyes, and then it seemed as if the cell was filled with men, strange men, who carried their heads in their left hands, and carried them by the mouth, because the hair was cut off. All shook their fists at me except the parricide.

I shut my eyes in horror, and saw it all the more distinctly.

Dream, vision, or reality, I should have gone mad if something had not aroused me from my paroxysm; I was in the act of falling backwards, when I felt a cold body with hairy feet walk over my foot. It was the spider whose web I had destroyed, and who was escaping. This brought me to my senses, but oh, what terrible apparitions!

No, no! it was imagination engendered by the working of my brain. The dead are dead, these especially, and fastened down securely in their tombs. That is a prison from which there is no escape. How could I be so frightened? The gates of the tomb do not open on this side.

CHAPTER XIII.

I have witnessed a horrible scene to-day.

It was bright daylight, and the prison was full of unaccustomed noise. I could hear the opening and shutting of heavy doors, the creaking of bolts and padlocks, the jingling of the keys that the warders carried at their waists, the shaking of the stairs under the tread of heavy feet, and voices calling to and answering each other, down the long corridors. My neighbours in the cells, the refractory convicts, were gayer than usual. All through Bicêtre rang the sound of mirth, and dance, and song.

I alone in the midst of all this hubbub was dumb. Not understanding the cause, I listened attentively.

One of the gaolers passed my door.

I ventured to ask him if there was a holiday in the prison.

"You may call it one if you like," replied he. "To-day they are putting irons on the convicts, who will start for Toulon to-morrow. Would you like to see it done?"

After the hermit's life that I had led such an offer was too good to be refused, odious as the spectacle might be, and I accepted his offer gratefully.

The warder took the usual precautions to ensure my safety, and then he conducted me to an empty cell, without an atom of furniture in it, but with a window, a real window, from which, though strongly barred, a glimpse of the sky could be caught.

"Here you are," said he; "from this you can both see and

hear; you have your private box just like a king!"

Then he left me alone, noisily securing the door with bolts, bars, and padlocks.

The window looked into a large square courtyard, round the four sides of which was a tall stone building six storeys in height. Nothing could look more miserable and naked than these buildings, pierced with an immense number of windows, all of them heavily barred. Every window was filled with a crowd of heads, piled one upon another like the stones that composed the walls, and framed as it were by the interlacing of the iron bars. These were the prisoners, spectators of a ceremony in which one day they would play the principal part. You could compare them to nothing but the souls in purgatory gazing through the windows that looked on to the infernal regions.

All gazed in silence on to the court, which was totally unoccupied.

In one of the buildings that surrounded the courtyard was an opening closed by a gate of iron bars; this opened into a smaller courtyard, surrounded, like the other, by a series of gloomy-looking buildings. All round the larger court were stone benches, built against the wall, and in the centre was a tall iron lamp-post.

Twelve o'clock struck; the gate was hurriedly thrown open. A waggon, escorted by men somewhat resembling soldiers, but dirty and untidy-looking, lumbered heavily into the yard with a loud clanking of iron. The men were the guardians of the galleys, and the waggon contained the chain.

At this moment, as if the noise had galvanized the prison into life, the spectators at the windows, who had up to this time preserved a strict silence, burst into cries of joy, into songs, oaths, and insults, mingled with peals of strident laughter heart-rending to hear. You would have imagined that it was an assembly of demons—on each face appeared a fiendish grin, fists were shaken through the window bars, every throat gave utterance to a yell, every eye flashed fire.

However, the escort proceeded to work at once. Amongst them I noticed several persons whom curiosity had led to the spot, and who now appeared to half repent of their temerity. One of the guards clambered on to the waggon and threw down to his comrades the chains, the travelling collars, and huge bundles of canvas trousers. Then each man proceeded to perform his allotted task; some laid out the chains against the walls, others arranged the shirts and trousers in heaps, whilst the more sagacious amongst them, under the guidance of their chief, a short, square-built man, carefully tested the iron collars to see that there were no flaws in them. All this was done in the midst of a flood of ribaldry from the prisoners, whose voices were occasionally drowned by the loud laughter of the convicts for whom these preparations were being made.

When these preliminaries were completed, a gentleman in a laced uniform, who was termed the inspector, gave an order to the governor of the prison; and a moment afterwards, through two or three low doors, rushed a yelling crowd of hideous and disgusting-looking men—these were the convicts.

Then the excitement of the lookers-on rose to its highest pitch. Those amongst the convicts who had earned a high criminal reputation were received with loud applause, which they acknowledged with a kind of haughty modesty. Many of the convicts carried in their hands hats which they had made from the straw supplied to them for bedding. One young man, or rather a boy, for he could not have been more than seventeen years of age, was much applauded. He had made himself an entire garment of straw, and came bounding into the yard, turning a succession of somersaults. He was as lithe and active as a serpent, and had been condemned to the galleys for theft. On his appearance there was a frenzied clapping of hands, and loud shouts of admiration. It was a frightful thing to witness this interchange of compliments between the veritable convicts and the aspirants to that distinction. As they came into the yard they were pushed and hustled between a double rank of the guards of the galleys in anticipation of the medical inspection. Then were the last efforts made to avoid the dreaded galleys, some pretending that they were lame, others that their eyesight was defective, and a hundred other excuses. But in most cases they were found to be in quite good enough health for the galleys, and they resigned themselves at once to their fate with utter carelessness, appearing entirely to forget the pretended ailments of a lifetime. The iron barred gate of the little court was now opened, and one of the guards commenced calling the roll, which was arranged alphabetically; and each convict, after answering his name, took up a position by the side of the comrade whom the chance of the initial letter had designated as his companion. Thus, if a convict had a friend, the odds were that he would be separated from him and linked to an unknown—another addition to their punishment.

When about thirty had been collected, the gate was again closed. One of the guards, forming them into line with blows of his stick, threw before each one a coarse shirt and a pair of trousers, and at the word of command they began to undress. And now a fresh and unexpected torture began. Up to this time the weather had been very fine; and if the October breeze was a little cold, still the rays of the sun were very grateful. But scarcely had the convicts removed their prison rags, and whilst the suspicious guards were examining them as they stood bare and naked before them, than the sky clouded over, and a heavy shower descended, flooding the courtyard with torrents of rain.

In the twinkling of an eye every one except the guards and the galley-slaves had left the courtyard, and had sought shelter under the gateways.

The rain still continued to fall, and nothing was to be seen but the naked bodies of the convicts glistening in the wet. A gloomy silence had succeeded their boastful fanfaronades. They shivered, and their teeth chattered; their emaciated legs and knotty knees trembled beneath the weight of their bodies, and it was pitiable to see them wrap the sodden shirts around their limbs, which were blue with the cold. Shirts and trousers were alike dripping with the rain; nudity would have been preferable to such a covering. One convict only, an elderly man, preserved his gaiety, complaining that "this was not in the programme." He endeavoured to dry his soaking shirt, and shook his fist at the clouds.

When they had put on their travelling garb, they were collected in parties of twenty or thirty into the corners of the yard where the chains had been deposited. The chains were long and massive, and at every two feet were two shorter transverse ones terminating in a collar, which was rivetted on the neck of the galley-slave during his journey to his destination. When these chains were spread along the ground they resembled the backbone of some huge fish.

The convicts were now ordered to sit down on the muddy

pavement; the collars were fitted to their necks; then the blacksmiths, carrying a portable anvil, fixed the rivets with heavy blows of a sledge-hammer.

This was a terrible moment; even the boldest amongst the convicts changed colour.

Every blow of the hammer as it fell on the anvil made the chin of the patient quiver; the slightest movement either forwards or backwards would have crushed the skull like a nutshell.

When this operation had been concluded, an appearance of gloom came over them; nothing could now be heard except the clanking of the chain, and at intervals a cry, and the sound of a blow, as the canes of the guards fell heavily upon the refractory convicts. Some of them wept, some trembled and bit their lips. I gazed with terror upon all these sinister faces in their iron frames.

So there were three acts in this lugubrious drama—the visit of the doctors, the visit of the gaolers, and the fixing of the chain. Suddenly a ray of sunlight appeared. From the conduct of the convicts it would have seemed that this gleam of light had set every brain on fire. They sprang to their feet with an unanimous effort. The five chains of criminals joined hands, and whirled in a mad dance round the lamp-post in the centre of the court, until the brain grew dizzy with watching their evolutions. They shouted out a song of the galleys, a slang romance set sometimes to a plaintive air, and at others to a gay and rollicking tune. Loud cries were heard, the panting of overtasked chests, and every now and then mysterious words were interchanged. The clanking of the chains served as the orchestra for the song, in itself more discordant than its accompaniment. Should I have desired to see a representation of the revels of demons, I could not have selected a better or a worse example.

Large buckets were then brought into the courtyard. The guards broke up the convicts' dance with blows and curses, and forced them to the buckets, in which I could see a few herbs swimming in some dirty smoking liquid.

Then they sat down and ate.

After having finished their meat they threw what remained upon the pavement, and recommenced their songs and dances. It is the custom to relax discipline a little during the day and the night upon which the chain is fastened on.

I was gazing upon this strange spectacle with so greedy a curiosity, and was watching its every phase with such attention, that I absolutely forgot myself. A deep feeling of pity crept over me, and their hollow laughter made me feel inclined to weep.

All of a sudden, in the midst of the sad reverie into which I had fallen, I saw the ring of dancers stop short, become perfectly silent, and then I noticed that every eye was fixed upon the window at which I was standing.

"The condemned man! the condemned man!" exclaimed they. Every finger was pointed at me, and the shouts of diabolical laughter were redoubled.

I was paralyzed. I could not understand how they could know me, how they could have recognized me.

"Good-day! good-day!" they cried, in piercing accents.

One of the youngest of the band, condemned to the galleys for life, gazed upon me with an envious look, and shouted, "Ah, you are in luck, for you will be sliced! Farewell, comrade."

I hardly know how I felt. It was a fact, I was their comrade, for the Place de Grève is the sister of the Galleys of Toulon; I even occupied a higher position than they did, and they paid me homage. I shuddered at the idea.

Their comrade—yes, and a few days later I should in my turn furnish a spectacle for men of their stamp.

I had remained spell-bound at the window, motionless, and unable to collect myself; but when I saw the five chains rushing towards me with expressions of fiendish cordiality, when I heard the clash of their chains and the tramp of their footsteps close to the wall, it seemed to me as if a crowd of demons were about to storm my wretched cell. I uttered a loud cry, and cast myself with violence against the door; but there was no means of escape, for it was securely bolted without. I pressed against it, I cried out in mingled terror and rage. I seemed to hear the hated voices of the convicts drawing nearer and nearer; I fancied that I could perceive their hideous heads appear above the window-sill. I uttered another cry of terror, and I fainted.

CHAPTER XIV.

When I came to myself it was night; I was lying on a truckle-bed. By the light of a lamp which hung from the ceiling I could see other beds placed in lines. Then I understood that I had been brought to the hospital.

For a few seconds I remained still; I was awake, but without consciousness or recollection. At any other time this hospital bed in the midst of a prison would have made me recoil with disgust, but I was no longer the same man. The sheets were coarse to the touch, and of a grey hue; the counterpane was thin and ragged; you could feel the palliasse through the mattress. But what did that matter? My limbs could stretch themselves freely between the coarse sheets, and the bed-clothes, thin as they were, drove away that terrible cold which seemed to freeze my very marrow. After a short interval I went to sleep again.

A great disturbance awoke me. It was broad daylight. The noise came from the outside. My bed was next to a window; I raised myself up to see what was the cause of the noise.

The window looked upon the main courtyard of the Bicêtre. It was crowded; a body of pensioners had great difficulty in keeping open a narrow path through the centre of the populace. Between a double rank of soldiers five long waggons, filled with men, jolted heavily along. The convicts were starting for their destination.

The vehicles had no covering. Each chain occupied one; the convicts were seated on a bench running down the centre, back to back, with the chains between them, and at the end stood a soldier with a loaded musket. You could hear their chains clank with every jolt, and their legs shake as they dangled over the side of the cart.

A fine searching rain was falling, chilling the air, and making their thin clothes cling to their limbs; their long beards and short hair were saturated with moisture, their faces were violet with the cold; I could see them shiver, and hear their teeth chatter with cold, and impotent rage.

Once riveted to the chain, a man ceased to exist as a separate individual. He must relinquish his intelligence, for the collar of the galleys condemns him to a living death, and, like a mere animal, he can only partially satisfy his appetite at given hours.

Motionless, the majority of them half-naked, with bare heads and dangling feet, they commenced their journey of twenty-five days' duration. Crowded together in the carts, garments of the same texture serving them as a defence against the scorching sun of July and the cold rains of November, it almost seemed as if man were endeavouring to press the elements into the post of executioner. The five waggons, escorted by cavalry and infantry, passed in turn through the main gateway of the Bicêtre; a sixth followed, in which were heaped together small boilers, copper vessels, and spare chains. A few of the guards who had lingered in the canteens hurried to gain their posts; the crowd melted away, and all the ghastly sight vanished like a dream of the night.

The sound of the wheels and the tramp of the horses grew fainter and fainter on the paved road that leads to Fontainebleau; the cracking of whips, the clink of chains, and the shouts of the populace as they wished the galley-slaves a prosperous journey, all died away. And for them this was only the beginning.

What was it my counsel said to me?

The galleys!

Ah, yes, death a thousand times sooner than that. Annihilation rather than hell. Sooner give my head to the knife of Guillotine, than my neck to the galley-slave's collar. The galleys, just Heaven, never!

CHAPTER XV.

Unfortunately I was not ill; the next day I had to leave the hospital, and once more I was relegated to my cell. Not ill! In point of fact, I am young, vigorous, and healthy. The blood flows freely in my veins, my limbs are under perfect control, I am strong in body and in intellect, made for a long life, and yet I am suffering from a mental disease, a disease the work of men's hands.

Since I left the hospital, an idea has crept into my brain—an idea which, when I think of it, almost drives me mad. It is, that if they had left me there I might have managed to escape. The doctors and the Sisters of Mercy seemed to take a great interest in me; I was so young for such a terrible death. One would have said that they pitied me, so eager were they to crowd round my bed. Bah! it was mere curiosity; and though these people would cure you of a fever, yet they would not cure a judicial sentence of death. And yet how easy it would be!—just an open door; and what harm would it do them? No more chance for me now; my appeal will be rejected, for everything has been done according to rule: the witnesses have testified correctly, the counsel have pleaded well, and the judges have done their part as they should. I cannot calculate on anything, unless—— No! it is madness, there is no more ground for hope. An appeal is a cord by which you are suspended over an abyss; you can hear it cracking a long time before it breaks and lets you fall. It is as though the knife of the guillotine took six weeks in which to fall.

If I could only gain my pardon—gain my pardon; but how, and for what reason? It is impossible for them to pardon me. All say that an example must be made.

I have but three steps to take—Bicêtre, the Conciergerie, and the Grêve.

CHAPTER XVI.

Oh, if I could only escape, how I would fly across the fields! Ah, but I must not run—that would draw attention and make people suspicious. On the contrary, I must walk slowly, with my head up, humming a tune. I ought to have an old handkerchief round the lower part of my face, a blue one with a pattern in red on it. It is a capital disguise, all the market-gardeners in the suburbs wear them. I know of a little clump of trees near Arcueil, by the side of a marsh. Once when I was at school I came there with my playmates to fish for frogs; I would hide myself there until night.

When it grew dark I would recommence my journey. I would go to Vincennes; no, the river is in the way, I will go to Arpajon. Perhaps it would be better to go by St. Germain, and get to Hâvre,—from thence I could embark for England. Well, I come to Longjumeau; a policeman passes me, he asks for my passport——I am lost!

Ah! hapless dreamer, first break through the three-foot wall that surrounds you. Death! Death!

I recollect when I was quite a child they brought me to Bicêtre to see the great wall, and the mad people.

CHAPTER XVII.

Whilst I am writing this my lamp has grown dim; the day is breaking, and the chapel clock has just struck six.

What does this mean—the warder has come into my cell, he has taken off his cap, and, softening his rough voice as best he can, has asked me what I should like for my breakfast?

A shiver runs through me.

Is it to be done to-day?

CHAPTER XVIII.

Yes, it is for to-day. The governor of the prison has been here, and has expressed his desire to serve me; has asked if I have any complaints to make about him or his subordinates; has inquired with much interest after my health, and how I have passed the night, and on leaving me called me *Sir*! It *is* for to-day.

CHAPTER XIX.

This gaoler does not believe that I can have any fault to find with him or with his subordinates. He is right; it would be ungracious of me to complain—they have but done their duty. They have guarded me well, and they have been courteous on my arrival, and on my departure. Ought I not to be satisfied? This good gaoler, with his calm smile and soothing words, with an eye that flatters whilst it watches, with his large and powerful hands, he is the incarnation of a prison—a Bicêtre transformed into a man. Everything around me reminds me of a prison; I recognize it in everything, in the human figure, as in the iron bars and bolts: this wall is a prison in stone, this door a prison in wood, these turnkeys are prisoners in flesh and bone. The prison is a kind of horrible being complete and indivisible, half building and half man. I am its victim; it grasps me, it wraps me in its folds, it shuts me up in its granite walls, it padlocks me with its iron bolts, and it watches me through the eyes of its gaolers.

Ah! unhappy wretch that I am, what is to become of me, *what are they going to do with me?*

CHAPTER XX.

I am calm again. All is over, and well for me that it is so. I am relieved from the terrible weight of suspense by the visit of the governor. For I confess it freely, I had hoped—now I hope no longer.

This is what has taken place.

Just as half-past six struck—no, it was a quarter to seven—the door of my cell opened, and an old white-haired man appeared on the threshold; he threw open his great-coat, and I saw from his gown that he was a priest.

This priest was not the chaplain of the prison, and this looked bad for me.

He sat down opposite to me, shook his head, and raised his eyes to heaven—that is, towards the roof of my cell. I understood what he meant.

"My son," said he, "are you prepared?"

In a feeble voice I replied, "I am not prepared, but I am ready."

But my sight grew dim; a cold sweat burst out upon me. I felt my temples swell, and there was a loud murmuring sound in my ears.

Whilst I swayed backwards and forwards in my chair like a man asleep, the good old man was talking—at least I suppose that he was, for I could see his lips move, his hands wave, and his eyes shine.

The door opened for the second time; the sound of the withdrawal of the bolts roused me from my stupor. This time it was the governor accompanied by a gentleman in a black coat, who bowed to me on entering; he held a roll of papers in his hands, and had about him that false air of sorrow which we see amongst undertakers.

"Sir," said he, "I am one of the ushers of the Courts of Justice: I have the honour to be the bearer of a message from the Public Prosecutor."

The first shock was over; all my presence of mind came back to me.

"The Public Prosecutor demands my head at once—is it not so?" asked I. "What an honour for me that he should write to me! I trust that my death will give him great pleasure, for he worked with too much ardour for it to have been a matter of indifference to him." Then in a calmer tone I added, "Read, sir."

Then he began a long rigmarole, intoning the last word in each sentence. This was the rejection of my appeal.

"The sentence will be executed on the Place de Grêve," added he, as he finished, without raising his eyes to mine. "We leave at half-past seven precisely for the Conciergerie, my good sir; will you have the extreme kindness to follow me?"

For the last few moments I had not been listening to him; the governor was talking to the priest, the usher's eyes were on his papers, whilst mine were fixed upon the door which had remained half opened. Ah! wretch that I am, there were four soldiers in the passage.

The usher repeated his question, this time looking full at me.

"Whenever you wish," answered I. "Suit your own convenience."

He bowed, and replied that he would call for me in half an hour! Then they went out, and left me alone.

Oh for some means of escape! O heavens, is there no hope? I must escape, I must on the spot—by the doors, by the windows, by the roof, even if I leave remnants of my flesh on the rafters and the joists.

Oh! horror, devils, curses, with good tools it would take me a month to pierce these walls, and I have not even a nail to work with or an hour to spare.

CHAPTER XXI.

FROM THE CONCIERGERIE.

Here I am *transferred*, as the order words it. But the journey is worth the trouble of relating. Half-past seven had just struck, as the usher again presented himself at the door of my cell.

"Sir," said he, "I am waiting for you."

Me—yes, and thousands of others.

I got up, and made a step towards him; it seemed as if I could not take a second, so heavy was my head, and so weak my legs. However, I made an effort, and advanced tolerably firmly. Before leaving I gave a farewell glance at the cell. I had grown to love it; besides, I left it empty, and open, which gave it a novel aspect. It will not long be so; another tenant is expected this evening—so the turnkey says, for the Court is now sitting, and conviction is certain.

At the end of the passage the chaplain came to take leave of me; he had been to breakfast. At the exit from the gaol the governor shook me affectionately by the hand, and reinforced my escort with four soldiers.

From the door of the hospital a dying man called out "*Au revoir.*" We were in the courtyard; I drew a long breath, it did me good.

We were not in the open air for long: a carriage was waiting for us—it was the same which had brought me here; it was oblong in shape, and divided into two compartments by iron bars standing so closely together that they appeared to be interlaced. Each section had a door, one in front, and one behind. The vehicle was so dirty and dusty, that the hearse which conveys paupers to their last resting-place is a state carriage in comparison to this one. Before burying myself in this tomb, I cast one glance round the courtyard, one of those despairing looks before which walls should crumble. There were many spectators waiting for my departure, more than there had been to look at the galley-slaves. As on that day a light rain was falling, and would no doubt fall all day—the shower would last longer than I should. The roads were much cut up, and the courtyard full of dirt and water. It was pleasant to see the crowd tramping about in the mud.

We got into the carriage—the usher and the soldiers in front; the priest, a policeman, and myself in the hindmost compartment.

Four mounted gendarmes surrounded the carriage; thus, without counting the driver, there were eight men to guard one poor wretch. As I got in I heard an old woman say, "Well, for my part I prefer *that* to the galley-slaves' chain."

I understood her—the sight was simpler, more easy to be taken in at a glance.

The carriage started; I heard the echoing sound as it rolled under the main portal of the Bicêtre, whose heavy gates closed behind us. I felt stupefied, like a man who has fallen into a trance, who can neither stir nor cry out, though he knows that they are burying him alive.

I listened dreamily to the jingle of the bells in the horses' collars, the rolling of the wheels, and the cadenced trot of the escort's horses, and the crack of the driver's whip. It seemed as if I was being carried away in a whirlwind.

Through the bars of a window in front of me my eyes caught an inscription in large letters over the Bicêtre—*Hospital for the Aged*.

"Ha!" exclaimed I, "it appears then that *some* people do grow old there."

All at once the vehicle made a sudden turn, which changed the scene. Now I saw the towers of Notre Dame rising through the mist of Paris.

"Those who have a place in the tower where the flagstaff is will have a good view," thought I.

I think that it was about this time that the priest began talking again. I let him go on without interruption; my ears were filled with the noise of the wheels, the horses' hoofs, and the coachman's whip—what mattered a little more noise?

I listened then to this flow of words, which soothed my feelings, like the murmur of falling water, when the sharp voice of the usher broke the silence.

"Well, Abbé," exclaimed he, "what news have you to-day?"

The chaplain, who had never ceased talking to me, made no reply.

"*Hé, hé!*" resumed the usher, raising his voice to drown the sound of the wheels, "what an infernal carriage this is!"

Infernal, indeed, for I found it so.

He continued: "It is the jolting and the rumbling, no doubt, that prevents your hearing me—what was I saying? Ah! your reverence, have you heard to-day's news that is exciting all Paris?"

I trembled; was he speaking of me?

"No," answered the priest, who had at last heard him, "I have not had time to read the morning papers; but I suppose I shall see it all in the evening. When I am much engaged, I tell our porter to keep them for me, and I read them on my return."

"What!" exclaimed the usher; "is it possible that you have not heard the news of this morning—the news that is convulsing Paris?"

I interrupted him.

"I think that I know it."

The usher stared at me.

"You! well, really, what do you say to it?"

"You are too curious," replied I.

"Why so, sir?" answered the usher. "Every one has his own opinion regarding politics, and I respect you too much not to presume that you have yours. For my part I am entirely in favour of the reconstruction of the National Guard; I was the sergeant of my company, and faith, it was most pleasant——"

I interrupted him again.

"It was not that I had imagined which caused the excitement, but something else."

"What was it then? You said you knew it."

"I was referring to something else that Paris was thinking of to-day."

The idiot did not yet understand me.

"Some more news! How on earth did you manage to pick them up? Can you guess what it can be, your reverence? Come, pray let me know. You cannot imagine how fond I am of a piece of news. I will repeat it to the President, it will amuse him."

And he uttered a hundred more platitudes, turning to the priest and to myself. I shrugged my shoulders.

"Well," continued he, "what are you thinking of?"

"I was thinking," answered I, "that I shall think no more this evening!"

"Ah! that is what is troubling you; you are cast down. Come, cheer up; Mr. Castaing talked all the way."

Then, after a pause, he continued: "I escorted Mr. Papavoine; he wore his otter-skin cap, and smoked all the way. As to those young people from Rochelle, they talked to each other the whole time."

"Madmen, enthusiasts," he added, "they appeared to despise all the world; but really, my young friend, you are too sad."

"Young!" answered I, bitterly; "I am older than you. Each quarter of an hour as it passes adds a year to my age."

He turned round and looked at me for a few seconds with unfeigned surprise.

"You are joking—older than I am; why I might be your grandfather."

"I was not joking," answered I, gravely.

He opened his snuff-box.

"There, my dear sir, do not be angry, and do not bear me a

grudge."

"I shall not bear it long," was my reply.

At this moment the snuff-box, which he had placed against the barred division, was shaken from his hand by a violent jolt of the vehicle, and fell at his feet.

"Confound the bars!" cried he. "Am I not unlucky? I have lost all my snuff!"

"I am losing more than you," answered I, with a smile.

He endeavoured to pick up the snuff, grumbling to himself.

"Losing more than me! that is easy to say; not a grain of snuff until I get to Paris; it is awful!"

The chaplain condoled with him on his loss; and, whether it was that I was preoccupied or not, I do not know, but it seemed to me as if this consolation fitted very well with the exhortation that he had commenced to me.

Little by little the conversation between the priest and the usher increased, whilst I buried myself in my own thoughts.

As we passed the barrier, the noise of the great city seemed louder than usual.

The vehicle stopped a moment at the office of the Customs whilst the officers examined it. If it had been an ox or a sheep that was being taken to the slaughter-house a fee would have to have been paid, but man goes free.

The boulevard once passed, we plunged into those old winding streets of the Cité and the Faubourg St. Marceau, which intersect each other like the paths of an ant-hill. On the stone-paved roadway of their streets the noise of the vehicle was so deafening that it drowned all exterior sounds. When I glanced through the little window it seemed to me as if the passers-by stopped to gaze after the carriage, whilst crowds of children followed at a run. At the crossings I could see ragged men and women holding in their hands bundles of newspapers which were eagerly purchased by the crowd.

Half-past eight sounded from the palace clocks as we arrived in the courtyard of the *Conciergerie*. The sight of the wide staircase, the gloomy chapel, and the sinister-looking wickets froze my blood. When the carriage stopped, I thought that my heart too would stop beating.

I summoned up my courage. The door was thrown open like a flash of lightning; I leapt from my rolling dungeon, and found myself under an archway between two ranks of soldiers. A curious crowd had already collected to watch my arrival.

CHAPTER XXII.

As long as I walked through the public passages of the Courts of Justice, I felt almost free and at my ease, but my courage almost failed me when a low door opened, and I was led through gloomy corridors and down secret staircases—places where only the condemned and their judges are permitted to enter.

The usher was still with me. The priest had left me promising to return in two hours, as he had some business to do.

I was led to the offices of the governor, to whom the usher handed me over. After all it was a mere exchange, for the governor begged him to wait for a few moments, as he had some *game* to give him which was to be taken back to the Bicêtre at once. No doubt this was the newly-condemned criminal; he who was to sleep in my cell upon the truss of straw which I had hardly used.

"Good!" answered the usher, "I will wait a moment, and we can draw up the documents for both of them at the same time."

Whilst this was being done I was placed in a small room adjoining the director's office, the door of which was securely fastened.

I do not know how long I had been there, or, indeed, of what I was thinking, when a violent burst of laughter close to my ear aroused me from my reverie. I started and looked up; I was not alone, there was a man with me—a man of about fifty-five years of age, of middle height, wrinkled, bent, and grey-haired, strongly built, with a sinister expression in his eyes, and a mocking smile upon his lips, dirty, ragged, and disgusting to the sight.

The door had been opened, and he had been thrust in without my having perceived it. Would death come thus to me?

This man and I gazed earnestly at each other for some moments, he continuing his sinister chuckle, which had something convulsive in it, and I half alarmed and wholly surprised.

"Who are you?" exclaimed I, at length.

"A nice question to ask," answered he. "I am *booked through*."

"What is that?" I inquired.

"It means," cried he, with another burst of laughter, "that in six weeks the knife will chop my nut into the sack, as it will yours in about six hours. Ha, ha! you understand me now, it seems."

He was right. I turned pale, and my hair stood on end, for

here was the other condemned man of to-day, my heir at the Bicêtre.

He continued—

"Well, this is my history. I am the son of a good old prig, and it was a pity that Charlot[1] strung him up by the neck: that was when the gallows was an institution. At six years of age I was an orphan, and used to pick up a few coppers in the spring by turning head over heels by the sides of the carriages. In winter I used to run about with my naked feet in the mud, blowing my fingers, all red with the cold, and showing my bare skin through the holes in my trousers. At nine I began to use my fingers, and from time to time I would empty a fob, or prig a cloak; and at ten I was a thoroughbred prig. Then I began to get pals round me. Atseventeen I was a cracksman and cracked a crib, but they caught me, and I was lagged. The galleys did not suit my complaint: black bread and cold water, a plank bed, and a cannon-ball to drag after me, not to mention blows of a stick, and a scorching sun; besides that they shaved me, and I used to have fine chestnut hair. But I did my time—fifteen years. I was thirty-two when they gave me the yellow passport and sixty-six francs, which I had earned during my fifteen years, working hard sixteen hours daily, thirty days in the month, and twelve months in the year. Well, there it was. I wanted to be an honest man with my sixty-six francs, and I had finer sentiments under my rags than you would find under many a priest's frock. But may the devil fly away with the passport, for it was yellow, and in it was written, 'Released Convict.'... I had to show that wherever I went, and to report myself every eighth day to the mayor of the village where they had assigned me a residence. An ex-galley-slave, a nice kind of recommendation! Every one shunned me; the little kids bolted when they saw me coming, and every door was shut in my nose. I could not get a day's work, and my sixty-six francs were soon eaten, and I wanted to live. I showed my strong arms, and offered a day's work for fifteen sous, for ten sous, for five sous, and could get nothing. What was I to do? One day, when I was hungry, I smashed a baker's window with my elbow and stole a loaf of bread. I was not allowed to eat the bread, but I was sent to the galleys for life, with a brand on my shoulders which I will show you if you like. And they call that justice. There I was, a returned lag. They sent me to Toulon, this time with a green cap.[2] I made up my mind to escape. I had three walls to break through, the chains to cut; but I had a nail to do it with. I escaped. They fired the gun, and all were on the alert. We are dressed in red like the cardinals, and they fire a salute when we go out. The powder went to kill the sparrows as far as I know. This time there was no yellow passport, and no money. I made my way back to some old pals who had done time themselves, and filled their pockets often enough. Their boss proposed a bit of high Toby. I was on like a shot, and I began to murder for a living. Sometimes it was a stage-coach, at others a post-chaise; sometimes a cattle merchant. We took their money, and we left the carriage and horses alone, and buried the man under a tree, taking care that his toes should not show; and then we jumped on the grave so that the newly-turned earth should attract no notice. I grew old at this game, hiding in the thickets—sleeping under the stars—tracked from wood to wood, but at least I was free. Everything comes to an end, however, and one day the slops put their fingers on my collar; my pals hooked it, and I remained with the chaps with the gold-laced hats. Well, they brought me here, I had climbed every rung of the ladder except one. I had got from prigging a wipe to cutting a throat, and there was no medium for me except the three-cornered knife. Well, well! my father had his cravat tied in public, and I shall make a first and last appearance in the Place de Grêve. That is all, my lad!"

I was horror-struck at his recital. He laughed louder than ever, and tried to take my hand. I shrunk away from him.

"My friend," said he, "you do not appear to have much pluck. Try and die game. You have a few unpleasant moments on the scaffold, but that is soon over. I wish that I could show you how to make the last jump properly. I should be glad if they would shave me as well as you to-day. The same priest would serve us both, and you might have him first if you like. You see that I am a good-natured devil."

He again made a step towards me.

"Sir," said I, pushing him back, "I thank you."

There was a fresh burst of laughter at my reply.

"Sir! Sir yourself if you come to that. Why, you must be a marquis at the least."

I interrupted him.

"Leave me alone, my friend; I want to collect myself."

The gravity of my speech made him serious for an instant. He shook his grey head, which was almost bald, and thrust his hand into his open shirt-front.

"I understand," muttered he; "you are expecting the parson."

Then after gazing at me for a few seconds—

"Look here," said he, timidly, "you are a marquis, that is all right; but you have a fine great-coat there, and it will not be of any use to you soon. Give it to me, and I will sell it for tobacco."

I took off my coat and gave it to him; he clapped his hands like a pleased child. Then, noticing that I was shivering in my shirt-sleeves, "You are cold," cried he; "it rains, and you will get wet. Put this on; besides, you ought to look respectable;" and whilst speaking, he took off his coarse woollen vest and thrust it into my hands.

I permitted him to do so, and then I leaned against the wall. I cannot tell you the effect that this man had on me. He had put on my great-coat, and was examining it with all attention, uttering every now and then cries of delight.

"The pockets are quite new," exclaimed he; "the collar is hardly soiled. I shall get at least fifteen francs for it. What happiness! tobacco for the next six weeks!"

Again the door opened. They came to take both of us away; to lead me to the chamber where the condemned await their last hour, and to remove him to the Bicêtre. He was placed in the midst of the escort, and went off laughing and saying—

"Now then, no mistakes. The gentleman and I have changed our skins, but I am not going to change places with him, now that I have tobacco for the next six weeks."

[1] The hangman
[2] The green cap was a sign of penal servitude for life.

CHAPTER XXIII.

The old scoundrel, he has taken my great-coat, for I did not give it to him, and he has left me this rag, this disgusting garment. What will people think of me?

Did I let him have my great-coat from carelessness, or from charity? Not a bit; but because he was stronger than I was, and had I not given it he would have beaten me with those sledge-hammer fists of his.

Not an atom of charity in it. I was filled with evil thoughts. I could have strangled the old thief; I could have trampled him under foot. I feel that my heart is full of rage and bitterness, as if my very gall-bladder had burst. Approaching death brings up many evil thoughts and feelings.

CHAPTER XXIV.

They have taken me into a bare cell, of course with any amount of bars in the windows and bolts on the door. I have asked for a table and a chair, and the means of writing. They have brought them. Then I asked for a bed. The gaoler cast a look of surprise upon me, which seemed to say, "What is the good of it to you?" However, they have arranged a trestle-bed in the corner; but at the same time a policeman has taken up his position in my room. Are they afraid that I shall strangle myself with the mattress?

CHAPTER XXV.

It is ten o'clock.

Oh! my poor little daughter, in six hours I shall be dead. I shall be a foul thing that they will lay upon the table at the College of Surgeons; upon one side they will take a mould of my head, upon the other they will dissect my body; then what remains of me they will put into a coffin, and expedite it to the cemetery of Clamont. That is what these men will do to your father. None of them hate me; all pity me, and all could save me; and yet they are going to kill me. Do you understand that, Marie? They will kill me in cold blood, in all due form, for the good that it will do. Oh, great heaven!

Poor little child! Your father who loves you so much, who kisses your little white and perfumed neck, who passes his fingers through the silky curls of your hair, who takes your sweet little face in his hand, who dances you on his knee, and at bedtime joins your little hands together, and teaches you to pray to God. Who will do this for you now? Who will love you? All children of your age will have fathers except you. How you will miss, my dear child, the New Year's gifts, the presents, the pretty play-things, the sugar-plums, and the kisses! You unhappy orphan, you may have to give up eating and drinking!

Ah! if the jury could only have seen my little Marie, they would have thought twice before killing the father of a child of three years old. And when she grows up, if she lives long enough, what will become of her? Her father will be one of the recollections of Paris. She will blush for me and my name. She will be despised and repulsed on all sides. Disgraced on my account who love her with all the tenderness of which my heart is capable. Oh, my well-beloved little Marie, can it be true that you will ever hold me in shame and horror?

Wretch! what crime have I committed, and what crime have I made society commit?

Can it be true that I shall be dead before the end of to-day? Is this really me? That dull sound that I hear outside, the crowds of people that are flocking along the quay, the gendarmes paraded in their barracks, the priest in his black robe, the man with the red-stained hands! Is all this for me? Is it I that am going to die—I, who am sitting here at this table, who lives, who feels, who breathes? Yes, it is I. I know it by the sense of touch, and by the creases I can make on my clothes.

CHAPTER XXVI.

I know something of it.

I was driving by the Place de Grève once, about eleven o'clock in the morning. All of a sudden the carriage stopped.

There was a crowd in the square. I put my head out of the door. Many women and children were standing in the parapets of the quay. Above their heads I could see a species of red scaffold which some workmen were putting together.

A man was to be executed that day, and they were erecting

the machine.

I turned away my head as this caught my eye. I heard a woman near me saying, "Look! the knife does not slide well, they are greasing the groove with a bit of candle!"

Probably they are doing that now. Eleven o'clock is just striking. No doubt they are greasing the groove.

Ah! miserable wretch, this time I shall not turn away my head!

CHAPTER XXVII.

Oh, my pardon, my pardon! perhaps I shall be reprieved. The king may interfere. Let them run and fetch my counsel to me; quick, my counsel! I choose the galleys; five years should settle it; or twenty years; or a brand with the red-hot iron: but let me have my life! A convict lives, moves, goes and comes, and sees the bright sun in the heavens.

CHAPTER XXVIII.

The priest has come back to me.

He has white hair, a gentle manner, and a benevolent face. Indeed, I have heard that he is a really good and charitable man. This morning I saw him distribute the contents of his purse amongst the prisoners. But his exhortations have no effect on me. I was callous to all that he could say, his words slided from my mind as cold rain from a frozen window-pane.

However, his reappearance gave me pleasure. Amongst all those who surround me, he is the only one who still looks upon me as a man, and I am thirsting for kind and cheering words.

We sat down, he on my chair, I on the bed.

"My son," commenced he. These words went at once straight to my heart. He continued, "Do you believe in God?"

"Yes, father," I replied.

"Do you believe in the Holy Roman Catholic and Apostolic Church?"

"Certainly," answered I.

"My son," observed he, "I fear that you are a waverer." Then he began to speak again. He talked for a long time; then when he fancied that he had said enough, he for the first time raised his eyes to mine as if to question me mutely.

"Well?" asked he.

I declare that I had listened to him first with eagerness, then with attention, and lastly with reverence.

I got up from my seat.

"Sir," said I, "leave me alone, I entreat of you."

"When shall I return?" asked he.

"I will let you know."

Then he left me without another word, shaking his head, as though he were saying to himself:

"An infidel!"

No, low as I have fallen, I am not an infidel. My God is my witness that I believe in Him. But what has this old man been able to say to me? Nothing that I have felt, nothing that has touched me, nothing that has drawn tears from my eyes, nothing which goes from his soul direct to mine. On the contrary, what he has said to me he might say to any one else, emphasizing his words when his argument had need of depth, full of platitudes when it should have been most simple, a kind of sentimental sermon and theological elegy. Here and there he put in a Latin quotation from Saint Gregory, Saint Austin, or some one else. He had the air of a man who repeats a lesson that he has said many times before, and which, though half forgotten and obliterated from his memory, returns again to him from the fact of his having known it long years before. There is no expression in his eye, no emphasis in his voice; nor do his features add to the power of his oratory.

And how could it be otherwise? This priest is the prison chaplain. His duty is to console and to exhort; he lives by that. He has grown old in preparing men for the scaffold. For many years he has made others tremble, whilst his white hairs never bristle at the horrors that he is a witness of. For him the scaffold and the galley are matters of every-day life. They bore him. Probably he keeps a book of sermons—such and such a page for those sentenced to death, and another for those in penal servitude. To-day he was warned that some one would require the consolations of religion. He asked whether it was a condemned criminal or a galley-slave, and, upon receiving the reply, turned to the necessary page, refreshed his memory, and came here.

Oh! if instead of sending for him they had sought out some young vicar, some old priest from a remote parish sitting in his chimney corner reading his book, and not expecting the summons; and saying to him: "There is a man about to die, come and console him. You will have to be with him when they bind his hands and cut his hair; you must ride in the cart with him, and with the crucifix hide the headsman from his sight; you will be jolting against him on the road to La Grêve; you will pass with him through the terrible crowd thirsting for his blood; you will take leave of him at the foot of the scaffold, and will remain in waiting until his head is in one place and his body in another."

Then when they bring me into his presence trembling from head to foot, when I embrace him and clasp his knees, he will weep; we shall mingle our tears together; he will wax eloquent, and I shall be consoled; my heart will soften to his words, he will take charge of my soul, and I shall rely on his God.

But this old man, what is he to me? What am I to him? A man of the lowest class, a shadow many of which he has seen, a mere unit added to the figures in the list of executions.

I was wrong, perhaps, to send him away as I did; it was he who behaved well, whilst I acted wrongly. It is my breath, that destroys and blasts everything around me.

They have brought me refreshment, fancying that I must be in need of it; a nice enough luncheon—a fowl, and something else, but after the first mouthful I have been unable to eat—everything tasted full of bitterness and corruption.

CHAPTER XXIX.

A man has just come in with his hat on; he produced a foot-rule from his pocket, and commenced measuring the stonework of the wall, murmuring to himself, "It is so;" and again, "No, that will not do."

I asked the gendarme who this was. It appears that he is a sort of assistant architect employed in the prison.

He seemed to feel some curiosity about me, for he whispered a few inquiries to the turnkey who accompanied him; then he fixed his eyes upon me, and, shaking his head in a careless manner, began to talk in a loud voice, and continued his measurements.

When his work was over he approached me, and said in a strident voice—

"My good friend, in six months this prison will be greatly improved."

But his manner seemed to imply, "It is a pity you will be unable to enjoy it."

He smiled blandly, and I really thought that he was going to rally me, as you might a young bride on her nuptial morning.

The gendarme in charge of me, an old soldier with several good-conduct stripes, took upon himself to reply.

"Sir," said he, "you must not talk so loud in the Chamber of Death."

The architect left the room, but I remained there as dumb as one of the stones that he had been measuring.

CHAPTER XXX.

Then a ridiculous incident occurred. The good old gendarme was relieved, and I, selfish wretch, had not even shaken hands with him. The new sentinel was a man of vulgar features, bull-eyed, with a foolish expression in his face.

I paid no attention to him. I had turned my back to the door, and, seated at the table, was pressing my hand to my forehead. A light tap upon my shoulder caused me to turn my head. The fresh guard and I were alone.

This is something the way in which he began the conversation, "Criminal, have you a kind heart?"

"No," answered I.

The sharpness of my reply seemed to disconcert him, but he began again after a moment's hesitation—

"But one is not wicked for the pleasure of being so!"

"Why not?" answered I. "If you have nothing better to say than that, leave me in peace. What are you aiming at?"

"Forgive me, criminal," replied he. "Suppose that you could ensure the happiness of a poor fellow without its costing you anything, would you not do so?"

I shrugged my shoulders.

"Have you come from a madhouse? You choose a strange moment to ask a favour. Why should I consult any one's happiness?"

He lowered his voice in a mysterious manner, which accorded ill with his idiotic expression.

"Yes, criminal, happiness for me, fortune for me, and all coming from you. Look here, I am a poor gendarme. The work is hard, and the pay light. The keep of my horse ruins me; so I put into the lottery to try and square myself. One must have an object in life. Up to this time I have failed to gain a prize because I have never chosen a lucky number. I seek for them in sure places, but am always a little wrong. If I stake on 76, 77 is sure to come up. I do all that I can, but the right one will never come up. A moment's patience, please; I am nearly at the end. Here is a lucky chance for me. It appears, criminal—forgive me—that it is all up with you to-day. It is a well-known fact that those who die as you do, see the lucky number in advance. Promise me that you will come to me to-morrow evening—it will be no trouble for you to do so—and to give me three numbers, three good ones. Will you, eh? I am not afraid of ghosts, so be easy. Here is my address: Cassine Popincourt, Staircase A, No. 26, at the bottom of the passage. You will remember that, will you not? Come this evening if that is more convenient."

I should have disdained to answer this fool, if a mad hope had not sprung up in my heart. In the desperate position in which I was placed, it seemed as if I might be able to break my chain with a slender reed like this.

"Listen," said I, playing my part as well as I could, "I can render you richer than a king; I can give you millions, on one condition."

He opened his dull eyes.

"What is it? what is it? anything that you wish."

"Instead of three numbers you shall have four. Change

clothes with me."

"Is that all?" exclaimed he, hurriedly unbuttoning his uniform.

I got up from my seat. I watched all his movements—my heart beat; already I saw all doors opening before the uniform of a gendarme, and the Conciergerie left far behind me.

Suddenly he stopped, with an air of hesitation. "Ah! you want to get out of this?"

"Of course," I replied; "but your fortune is made."

He interrupted me.

"Ah, no, that will not do; how could the numbers be worth anything if you were not dead?"

I sat down in silence; all hope had fled, and again I was plunged in despair.

CHAPTER XXXI.

I closed my eyes, and covered them with my hands, striving to forget the present in the past. As I pondered, the recollections of my childhood came back to me, soft, calm, and smiling like islands of flowers, in the black gulf of confused thoughts which turned and twisted in my brain.

I could see myself once again, a laughing schoolboy, playing, running, and shouting to my brothers, in the green avenues of the neglected garden of the home where my earlier years were spent. And then, four years later, I was there—still a child, but full of dreams and sentiments. But there was a girl with me in the lonely garden.

A little Spaniard, with large eyes and long hair, olive-tinted skin, red lips and cheeks, an Andalusian, fourteen years of age, called Pepa. Our mothers had told us to run about together in the garden; we came out and walked about. They had told us to play, but we preferred to talk, children of the same age but different sex.

For more than a year we had been in the habit of playing and quarrelling together. I disputed with Pepita for the ripest apple on the tree, and I once struck her for the possession of a bird's nest. She wept, and I said, "Serves you right," and we both ran to complain to our mothers, who openly blamed me, but in their inmost heart each thought that her own child was right.

Now she is leaning on my arm; I feel proud and happy. We are walking slowly, and conversing in low tones. She lets her handkerchief drop, I pick it up for her; our hands tremble as they meet. She is talking to me of the little birds, of the sun that we see over there setting in crimson behind the trees, of her schoolmates, of her dress, of her ribbons. We talk of the most innocent things, and yet we blush; the child has become a young girl.

It was a summer's evening; we were under the chestnut-trees at the bottom of the garden.

After one of those long intervals of silence which occurred so often in our walks, she suddenly let go of my arm, and cried, "Let us run." And she started off in front of me, her figure slender as a wasp's, her little feet raising her dress half-way up the leg. I pursued her; she fled. As she dashed along the wind raised her tippet, and showed the olive-tinted hue of her neck.

I was beside myself; I caught her just by the ruined well. As the winner I seized her by the waist, and drew her down upon a bank of turf. She was out of breath, and laughing. I was quite serious, and gazed into her dark eyes, half-veiled by her black lashes.

"Sit there," said she to me; "there is plenty of daylight, let us read. Have you a book?"

I had with me the second volume of the "Travels of Spalanzani." I opened it at hazard, and moved close to her; she rested her shoulder against mine, and we began to read upon the same page. Before turning the page she had always to wait for me. Her intellect ran quicker than mine did.

"Have you finished?" she asked, when I had hardly begun.

Our heads touched, our hair mingled together, and our respirations crossed each other, and then our lips met.

When we wished to begin reading again, the sky was studded with stars.

"Oh, mamma, mamma!" she exclaimed as she entered the house, "how we have been running!"

I kept silence.

"You say nothing, my boy," said my mother. "You look sad."

My heart was full of bliss.

I shall remember that evening until the last day of my life.

The last day of my life!

CHAPTER XXXII.

Some hour has struck—I do not know which. I can hardly hear the sound; there is a buzzing in my ears, it is my last thoughts that are working in my brain.

At this last moment I fall back upon my recollections. I look upon my crime with horror, but I wish for a longer time for repentance. I had more feelings of remorse before my condemnation; since, it seems that there is room for nothing except the thoughts of death. When my thoughts turn for a moment to my past life, they veer round to the axe which will shortly terminate all, and I shiver as if the idea was a new one. My happy childhood, my glorious youth, the end of which is to be stained with my blood. Between that and the present there is a river of blood, another's and mine. If any one ever reads my life, they will not believe in this fatal year, which opens with a crime, and closes with a shameful punishment. It would be impossible to credit it.

A sanguinary law, O cruel men—and yet I was not naturally wicked.

To die in a few hours, and to think that there was a time when I was free and pure, when I wandered under the trees, when I walked upon the leaf-strewn paths.

CHAPTER XXXIII.

At this very time there is, in the houses around the place in which I am, men who come and go, who laugh and talk, who read the paper and talk over their affairs, tradesmen who sell, young girls who are working at their ball-dresses, and mothers who are playing with their children.

CHAPTER XXXIV.

I recollect one day, when I was a child, going to see the peal of bells of Notre Dame. I was already dizzy with having mounted the dark winding staircase, and having crossed the narrow gallery which connects the two towers of the cathedral, and saw Paris stretching beneath my feet; then I entered the belfry where hangs the bell, and its clapper which weighs I know not how many pounds.

I advanced hesitatingly over the uneven flooring, gazing at the bell so celebrated amongst the children and the people of Paris, and remarked, not without a feeling of terror, that the sloping tile roofs were on a level with my feet; and I took a bird's-eye view of the place of Paris—Notre Dame, and the passers-by looking like a swarm of ants. All of a sudden the heavy bell rang, a vibration shook the air and made the lofty tower quiver. The planking trembled on the beams. Affrighted, I threw myself upon the flooring, and clasped it with my two hands, speechless and breathless, with that tremendous pealing in my ears, whilst under my very eyes was that tremendous precipice where so many people were passing in calm and quiet. Well, it seems that I am still in the belfry tower. Everything seems to be buzzing and humming around me, there is a sound of bells beating on my brain; and around me, as across an abyss, I can see that calm and peaceful life that I have quitted where men walk peacefully to and fro.

CHAPTER XXXV.

The Hotel de Ville is a sinister-looking edifice with its pointed roof, and its strange-looking clock with a white face, its staircases worn by the feet of many passers-by. There are two arches on the left and right. There it stands facing the Place de Grêve, sombre and melancholy, its front worn away by age, and so dark that even in the sunshine it looks black.

On the day of an execution gendarmes issue in crowds from all the doors, and its hundreds of windows gaze sternly upon the condemned man. In the evening the face of the illuminated clock shows brilliant against its gloomy walls.

CHAPTER XXXVI.

It is a quarter past one.

This is how I feel. A violent headache and cold in the extremities, and a burning forehead. Each time that I rise or bend it seems to me as if some liquid which floats in my skull drives my brain against the top of my head.

I have nervous tremblings, and every now and then the pen falls from my hands as though I had sustained a galvanic shock.

My eyes water as if I were in a smoky room.

I have a pain in my elbows.

But in two hours and forty-five minutes I shall be cured.

CHAPTER XXXVII.

There are those who say that the pain is nothing, that I shall hardly suffer at all, that science has made death very easy.

What then is this six weeks' torment that I have suffered, and this death agony for a whole day? What will be said of this day that goes so slowly, and yet too quickly? What is this ladder of torture that leads to the scaffold?

Perhaps they do not call this suffering.

Are not there the same convulsions when the blood oozes

out drop by drop, and the intellect weakens as each thought grows less coherent?

And so there is no suffering. Are they sure? Who has told them so? Has there ever been an instance of a severed head which has risen bleeding to the edge of the basket, and has cried to the populace, "It has not hurt me a bit!"

Have any dead returned to thank the inventor, and to say, "It is a splendid invention, the mechanism is good. Stick to it?"

No, nothing of the kind—in a minute, in a second the thing is done. Have they ever, even in thought, put themselves in the place of the criminal, when the heavy knife falls, bites into the flesh, grinds through the nerves and shivers the vertebræ? But all pain is over in half a second. Horror!

CHAPTER XXXVIII.

It is strange that I can think of nothing but the king. It is no use trying to drive it away; a voice in my ears keeps on crying: "At this very moment he is in this city, not far from here, in another palace—a man who, too, has guards at all his doors, a man in a similar position to yourself, except that he is in the highest whilst you are in the lowest. Every instant of his life is nothing but glory, grandeur, delight, and revelry. Around him congregate love, respect, and veneration. The loudest voice softens as it speaks to him, and the haughtiest heads incline. Gold and silk are ever before his eyes. Now he may be holding a council of his ministers, all of whom are of his opinion; or he may be going out hunting, and to a ball this evening, leaving to others the work of preparing his pleasures."

Well, this man is flesh and blood as I am, and one stroke of his pen would make this horrible scaffold disappear, and restore me to life, liberty, family, and wealth. And he is kind, they say, and would gladly do so; but yet nothing will be done.

CHAPTER XXXIX.

But let me be courageous with death, let me grasp the horrible idea and consider it face to face. Let us ask it what it really is, let it tell us what its wishes are; let us turn it over in every way and spell out the puzzle, gazing forwards into the tomb.

I imagine that when my eyes are closed, I shall see a bottomless abyss of light into which my soul will fall. I believe that the sky itself will be resplendent with light, and that the stars will be mere dark spots instead of being, as they are now, sparks of diamonds upon a canopy of black velvet.

Or perchance, miserable wretch that I am, I shall fall without cessation into the depths of a hideous black gulf, seeing hideous forms threatening me on all sides.

Or, after receiving the blow, shall I awake and find myself upon a soft flat surface, wandering about in semi-darkness, and turning over and over like a head that rolls? I can fancy that there will be a strong wind, and that my head will be jolted with other rolling heads. In places there will be brooks and ponds of an unknown liquid, but all will be black.

When, in the midst of my revolutions, my eyes will be turned upwards, they will look upon a sky of shadows, and far away in the background huge arches of smoke darker than the darkness itself. I shall see millions of red sparks flitting about, which upon coming near to me will turn into birds of fire;—and this will go on for ever and ever.

It may be that, upon certain gloomy nights of winter, those who have died upon the Place de Grêve may meet together, for is it not their domain? It will be a pale and bleeding crowd, and assuredly I shall not be absent from it. There will be no moon, and we shall all speak in a low voice. The Hotel de Ville will be there, with its mouldering walls, its dilapidated roof, and the clock that had no pity for us.

A guillotine from Hell will be erected, where a demon will execute a headsman. The hour will be four, and we shall form the crowd round the scaffold.

Probably things will be like this. But if the dead do return, in what shapes will they appear? What part of their incomplete and mutilated body will they keep? Which will they choose? Shall the head or the trunk appear as a spectre?

Alas! what has Death done with the soul? What feelings does it leave to it? What has it taken away, and what has it given? Where does he put it? and does he ever lend it the eyes of the flesh to look upon this earth and weep?

O for a priest, a priest who can tell me this;
I want a priest, and a crucifix to kiss,
Always the same, my God!

CHAPTER XL.

I have asked them to let me sleep a little, and have thrown myself upon the bed.

I have a rush of blood to the head, which makes rest necessary to me. This is my last sleep in this life. I have had a dream.

I dreamt that it was night, that I was in my study with two or three of my friends, whose names I do not recollect.

My wife was asleep in a room hard by, and our child was with her.

My friends and I spoke in a low voice, so that we might not alarm them.

All of a sudden we heard a strange noise in some other portion of the house; it was like a key being turned quietly, like the creaking of a bolt.

There was something in the sound that alarmed us. We imagined that it might be thieves who had got into the house.

We resolved to search the premises. I rose, took a candle in my hand; my friends followed me one by one. We passed through the bedroom where my wife was sleeping with our child by her side. Then we came to the drawing-room. There was no one there. The family portraits hung upon the wall, which was covered with red paper, motionless in their gilded homes. It seemed to me as if the dining-room door was not in its usual place.

We entered the dining-room, and searched it, I going first.

The door that led into the staircase was closed, and so were the windows. Near the stove I noticed that the linen-closet was open, and the door drawn back forming an angle with the wall, as though to conceal something.

This surprised us; we imagined that there was some one hiding behind the door.

I tried to close it, and experienced some resistance. In astonishment I pulled harder, when it yielded suddenly, and behind it we saw a little old woman standing motionless against the wall, her eyes closed, and her arms hanging down in front of her.

She looked hideous, and my hair bristled.

I said, "What are you doing here?"

She made no answer.

I asked, "Who are you?"

She did not reply, nor did she move or unclose her eyes.

My friends said, "No doubt she is in league with those who have broken into the house with some evil design. Upon hearing us coming they fled, but she having been unable to escape hid herself here."

I again questioned her, but she continued silent, motionless, and sightless.

One of my friends pushed her. She fell to the ground like a log, like some inanimate object.

We pushed her with our feet, then we raised her again, and stood her up against the wall; but she showed no sign of life, and remained dumb to our questions, as though she were deaf.

At last we lost patience; anger began to mingle with our fright.

One of us suggested—

"Put the flame of the candle under her chin."

I did so; then she half opened one eye, a vague, dull eye with no expression in it.

I moved away the candle, and said—

"Will you answer me now, you old witch?"

The open eye closed again.

"Ah, this is too much," cried the others. "Give her the candle again—she shall answer us."

I put the flame again under her chin.

Then she opened both eyes slowly, and gazed upon us all round; then, bending her head abruptly, she blew out the candle with a breath that froze like ice; and at the same instant I felt, in the darkness, three sharp teeth pierce my hand.

I woke trembling, and bathed in a cold perspiration. The good old priest was seated by my side reading his prayer-book.

"Have I slept long?" asked I.

"My son," replied he, "you have been sleeping an hour. They have brought your child to take leave of you, she is in the adjoining room. She is waiting for you, but I would not let them wake you."

"My child, my child!" I exclaimed; "bring me my child!"

CHAPTER XLI.

She is young and rosy, and has large eyes; she is a pretty child.

She wears a dear little dress that becomes her well.

I have taken her up in my arms, and placed her upon my knees, and kissed her hair.

Why is her mother not with her? She is ill, and her grandmother is ill too.

She gazed upon me with an air of astonishment; she permitted me to caress her, embrace her, and devour her with kisses, but from time to time she cast an uneasy look at her nurse, who was weeping in a corner of the room.

At last I was able to speak.

"Marie!" said I. "My little Marie!"

I pressed her tightly to my bosom; she pushed me away with a low cry.

"Oh, sir," said she, "you hurt me."

Sir! It was nearly a year since she had seen me. She had forgotten me. Words, face, speech, all were faded from her memory; and who would recognize me in this dress, with my beard and my livid complexion? Was I lost to the only one that I should have cared to remember me?

To be no more a father—to be condemned never to hear that word again from the lips of a child, that word which is so sweet, but which a man's tongue cannot frame, "Papa."

And yet to hear it once again from those lips, only once again, I would gladly have given the forty years of life that they were going to take away from me.

"Listen, Marie," said I, joining her two little hands in mine. "Do you not know me?"

She looked at me with her beautiful eyes, and answered—"No."

"Look at me well," urged I. "Now who am I?"

"You are a gentleman," replied she.

Alas! to love one creature so fondly in the world—to love her with all your passionate love, to have her with you to look into her eyes, and to hear her answer that she does not know you.

"Marie," continued I, "have you a papa?"

"Yes, sir," said the child.

"Well, where is he?"

She raised her great eyes full of wonder.

"Do you not know?" said she. "He is dead!"

Then she began to cry, and I almost let her fall.

"Dead," repeated I. "Marie, do you know what it is to be dead?"

"Yes, sir," answered she; "it is to be in the churchyard, and in heaven."

Then she continued, "I pray to the good God for him night and morning at mamma's knees."

I kissed her forehead.

"Marie, say your prayers."

"I must not, sir; prayers must not be said in the middle of the day; come this evening and I will say them to you."

This was too much, and I interrupted her.

"Marie, it is I that am your papa."

"Oh," answered she.

I added—

"Do you not wish that I should be your papa?"

I covered her with tears and kisses. She endeavoured to disengage herself from my embrace, crying—

"Your beard hurts me."

Then I put her once more upon my knees, and, looking into her eyes, asked her—

"Marie, do you know how to read?"

"Yes," answered she, "I can read; mamma taught me my letters."

"Come, read a little," said I, showing her a paper that she had crumpled up in her hand.

She shook her little head.

"I can only read fables," said she.

"Never mind, try, come, let us see."

She unfolded the paper, and began to spell it out, pointing to each letter with her finger.

"S, E, N, sen; T, E, N, C, E——"

I snatched it from her hand. It was the sentence of death that she was reading to me, and her nurse had bought the paper for a penny. It would cost me more than that.

No words can describe my feelings. My violence frightened the child. She almost wept. Suddenly she exclaimed, "Give me back my piece of paper; I want it for a plaything."

I gave her to the nurse. "Take her away," I cried. Then I fell back in my chair, gloomy, worn-out, and desperate. Let them come now, I care for nothing; the last link that binds me to life is broken, they can do what they like with me.

CHAPTER XLII.

The priest is kind, and the gaoler, too, has his tender side. I believe that they both shed a tear, as I told the nurse to take away my child.

It is over; now I have only to strengthen myself, and to think boldly of the executioner, of the cart, of the gendarmes, of the crowd on the bridge, of the crowd on the quay, of the crowd at the windows, and of that crowd which has assembled expressly for me on the Place de Grève, which might be paved with the heads that have fallen there. I think that I have a whole hour to accustom myself to these thoughts.

CHAPTER XLIII.

The multitude will laugh, will clap its hands, will applaud; and amongst all those free and unknown men, who hasten, full of pleasure, to an execution, in that crowd of heads that will cover the open space, there will be more than one predestined to follow mine sooner or later into the blood-stained basket. More than one who has come for me will one day come on his own account.

CHAPTER XLIV.

My little Marie, they have taken her back to her play; she will look at the crowd through the windows of the cab, and will think no more of *that gentleman*!

Perhaps I shall yet have time to write a few pages for her, that one day she will read; and fifteen years hence she may perhaps weep for to-day.

Yes, she must have from me my true story, and why my name has a stain of blood upon it.

CHAPTER XLV.

MY HISTORY.

Note by the Editor.—It has been impossible to find the manuscript to which this refers. Perhaps, as is indicated by those that follow, the idea came to him without his having had time to execute it. The time was short when he thought of it.

CHAPTER XLVI.

FROM A ROOM IN THE HOTEL DE VILLE.

From the Hotel de Ville!... I am there; the terrible journey has been made. *The place is there,* below my window. And the vile populace are there, hooting and laughing as they wait for me.

I had need to endeavour to pluck up courage, to strengthen

my nerves, for my heart failed me when I saw those two red posts, with the black triangle at their summit, erect themselves between the two lamp-posts on the quay. I demanded to be permitted to make a last declaration, and they brought me here, and have gone to find the Public Prosecutor. I am waiting for him; at any rate it is so much time gained.

Here it comes. They warn me that the time has arrived. I trembled, as though I had thought of nothing else for the last six hours, for the last six weeks, for the last six months. It came upon me as if it were something totally unexpected.

They have led me through their passages, and made me ascend and descend their staircases. They have pushed me through a folding-door into a room on the ground floor, dark and narrow, with a vaulted roof; the foggy, rainy day hardly allows any light to penetrate into it. A chair was standing in the centre; they told me to sit down, and I did so.

There were several people standing about besides the priest and the gendarmes; *there were also three men.*

The first was tall, old, and fat, with a red face, and he wore a great-coat and a broken three-cornered hat. *It was he!*

It was the headsman, the man of the guillotine; the others were his assistants.

Scarcely was I seated, than these two approached me from behind, stealthily as cats; then in a moment I felt cold steel in my hair, and heard the snipping noise of the scissors close to my ears.

Carelessly severed, my hair fell in masses on my shoulders, whilst the man in the three-cornered hat brushed them gently away with his large hand.

Every one round me whispered.

Outside there was a strange murmuring sound; at first I thought that it was the river, but from the laughter that arose from intervals, I knew it was the crowd. A young man seated near the window, who was writing with a pencil in a note-book, asked the men what they were doing.

"It is the last toilet of the condemned," was the reply.

I then understood that all this would be read to-morrow in the papers.

All at once one of the assistants took off my waistcoat, whilst the other seized my two hands and brought them behind my back, whilst I could feel a cord being knotted round my wrists. At the same moment the other took off my necktie. My linen shirt, a last relic of bygone days, seemed to make him hesitate for a moment; then he cut off the collar.

At this horrible moment, when the cold steel touched my neck, my elbow quivered, and I uttered a low moan of stilled rage. The executioner's hand shook.

"Sir," said he, "forgive me, have I hurt you?"

These executioners have excellent manners.

The crowd outside is yelling louder than ever.

The headsman pressed to my nostrils a handkerchief, strongly impregnated with aromatic vinegar.

"Thank you," said I, in as firm a voice as I could; "it is useless. I feel better."

Then one of them stooped to bind my feet together. This was done with a slender simple cord, which enabled me to take very short steps, and it was attached to the one that secured my wrists.

Then the big man threw the waistcoat on my back, tying the sleeves together under my chin. There was nothing more to be done

The priest now approached with the crucifix.

"Come, my son," said he.

The assistants put their hands under my arms, and I was lifted up. My steps were slow and tottering.

At the instant, the outer door was thrown wide open, and an irruption of noise, cold air, and blinding light burst in upon the gloom of the chamber. From the darkness I could see through the rain the thousands of heads, all shouting and yelling, piled one upon the other; on the right a line of mounted gendarmes; in front a detachment of infantry; on the left the back of a cart in which was a ladder—a terrible picture framed by the door of the prison. This was the dreaded moment for which I had nerved myself. I made two steps forward, and appeared on the threshold of the door.

"There he is! there he is!" cried the crowd; "he is coming at last!"

And those nearest to me clapped their hands. The king himself is not received with greater honours.

It was a mere ordinary cart, with a miserable hack in it, driven by a man in a blouse. The big man with the three-cornered hat mounted first.

"Good day, Monsieur Sanson," cried the children.

One of the assistants followed him.

"Good day, Tuesday," cried they once more.

Both of them took their place on the seat in front. Now it was my turn, and I mounted with a calm demeanour.

"He is going to die game," said a woman near the gendarmes.

This infamous praise gave me courage. The priest took his place by me. I was placed in the back seat, my face turned away from the horse. I shivered at this last act of attention. There was an air of humanity in it.

A squadron of gendarmes awaited me at the gate of the palace.

The officer gave the word of command, and the escort and the cart started with a roar of applause from the crowd.

"Hats off! hats off!" cried a thousand throats. It was as if the king was passing.

Then I laughed a ghastly laugh, and muttered to the priest, "Their hats, my head!"

We moved at a foot's pace.

There was a breath of perfume from the Flower Market; the stall-keepers had left their bouquets to come and see me. A little farther on there were many public-houses, the upper floors of which were full of spectators, rejoicing in the excellent places which they had secured. The women especially seemed delighted. They had hired tables, chairs, scaffolds, and carts to stand upon. Every coign of vantage bent beneath the weight of the spectators. The men who made their living by these spillings of human gore, cried at the top of their voices—

"Who wants a place?"

Hatred for this merciless crowd filled my heart, and I felt inclined to cry out, "*Who wants mine?*"

Still the cart went on; at each step the crowd disappeared from behind it, and I saw them re-form again farther on in front.

Upon passing the Pont de Change, I chanced to cast my eyes backwards on the right-hand side—I saw a tall black tower standing by itself, covered with carvings, upon the top of which sat two stone monsters. I had no reason for putting the question to the priest, but I asked, "What is that?"

"The tower of Saint Jacques la Boucherie," he replied.

We moved on slowly, the crowd was so great. I feared to show cowardice. Last remnant of vanity! Then I pulled myself together, and endeavoured to be blind and deaf to everything except the priest, whose words I could scarcely catch.

Then I took the crucifix in my hands, and kissed it.

"Have pity on me," cried I, "O my God!" and I endeavoured to busy myself in that thought. But each jolt of the clumsy vehicle scattered my thoughts. Suddenly I felt very cold; the rain had soaked through my clothes, and my head, deprived of the protecting hair, was quite wet.

"You are shivering with the cold, my son," remarked the priest.

"Yes," replied I. Alas! it was not the cold that I was shivering with.

At the end of the bridge some women pitied me because I was so young.

We reached the fatal quay. My sight and hearing grew dim once more; those voices, the heads at the windows, at the doors, in the shops, on the cross-bar of the lamp-posts, those eager and cruel spectators, those crowds who knew me, and amongst whom I knew no one, those lines of human faces——I was intoxicated, stupid, mad. So many eyes all fixed upon me became an unbearable torture.

I shook upon my seat, and paid no more attention to crucifix or priest.

In the tempest of sound that enfolded me I could no longer distinguish expressions of sympathy from jeers and insults; everything roared and resounded in my ears like the echo from a copper vessel.

Unconsciously I began to read the names over the shops. Once a feeling of morbid curiosity urged me to turn my head, and to look at what we were approaching.

It was the last bravado of the intellect—but the body would not obey it, for my neck remained stiff and obstinate.

I glanced to my left across the river; I could see one tower of Notre Dame, the other was hidden by it. It was the one upon which the flagstaff is. There was a great crowd upon it; they must have had a good view.

And the cart went on and on, and shop succeeded to shop, and the people laughed and stamped about in the mud; and I gazed calmly upon everything as people do in their dreams.

All of a sudden the row of shops upon which my eyes were fixed were cut by the corner of a square. The noise of the crowd became more sonorous, tumultuous, and merry. Suddenly the cart stopped, and I almost fell forwards.

The priest caught me by the arm.

"Courage," murmured he.

Then they brought a ladder to the back of the cart; an arm was stretched out to aid me in my descent. I took the first step, and attempted to take another—but it was useless, for on the quay, between two lamp-posts, I had caught sight of a terrible object.

It was the realization of all my terrors.

I staggered as though I had received a heavy blow.

"I have a last confession to make," muttered I, feebly. They brought me here.

I asked them to let me write. They untied my hands; but the cord is here, ready for me, and the other horror is below, waiting for me.

A judge, a commissioner, or a magistrate—I know not which—came to me. I asked for a pardon, clasping my hands, and kneeling to them. With a calm smile, they asked me if that was all I had to say.

"My pardon, my pardon," repeated I: "or five minutes' more life, for pity's sake! You do not know—it may be on its way, it may arrive at the last moment—such things have often been heard of before. And of what use will pardon be, sir, if I am no longer in a condition to benefit by it?"

That accursed executioner is whispering to the judge that it must be performed by a certain time, that the hour is at hand, and that he is responsible for its due performance; besides, it is raining, and there is a chance of *the thing* getting rusty.

"For mercy's sake! one minute more to wait for the coming of my pardon! If you will not grant it, I will defend myself tooth and nail!"

The judge and the executioner have left me. I am alone—alone with two gendarmes.

Oh the horrible crowd, with their hyena-like cries! How do I know that I shall not escape them—if I shall not be saved? My pardon may arrive——Ah, the wretches, they are carrying me on to the scaffold....

* * * * * *

FOUR O'CLOCK STRIKES.

www.ingramcontent.com/pod-product-compliance
Lightning Source LLC
Chambersburg PA
CBHW020213090426
42734CB00008B/1043